This Time Next Week

Motto: Royal Masonic School For Girls
Circumornatae ut similitudo templi
—Psalm 144 v12

That our Daughters may be as the polished
corners of the Temple
—Latin translation by St Jerome

This Time Next Week

THE ENGAGING STORY OF A LITTLE GIRL BROUGHT UP IN THE CARE OF THE FREEMASONS, BEFORE AND DURING WORLD WAR II

B J KELLAND

EPONA

First published 2005 by Epona

www.eponamedia.com

ISBN 0 9543099 2 8

A CIP catalogue record for this book is available from the British Library.

For my late Mother and all the Freemasons,
whose philanthropic spirit helped both of us so much.

PREFACE

October, 2004

One day during a conversation with a friend at work, I happened to mention that I had attended the Masonic School for Girls. Her reaction was predictable.

"Oh, so you were one of the privileged few," she said.

Without a moment's hesitation I replied, "Yes, we lost our fathers."

She remained silent.

Many years would pass before I recalled these words. I was getting ready to move house and had to face the unenviable task of clearing out the loft. And that was when I came across bundles of letters tied together with string. There were also several cardboard boxes and bags containing pieces of paper and official looking documents. They were all exactly where I had put them a good two decades earlier, in the same tea chest, placed in the loft after Mother died. For one reason or another, I simply had not found the emotional strength to go through all her belongings.

The letters were some of the ones I had written during my eleven years at both the junior and senior Masonic schools at Weybridge and Rickmansworth. I was suddenly curious to discover what I had said to Mother. Aged only seven, I had started writing a weekly letter home, forming a routine that was never broken. Many of the early letters are very short, just a few lines, in pencil. I was invariably asking Mother for something to be sent to me, like my stamp album, toothpaste or telling her how well I had done in arithmetic or the latest item I was making in handwork. Not earth shattering events in themselves, but important to Mother and me.

The pieces of paper and documents related to events that had taken place in Mother's life during the 1930s and 40s. Several concerned her widow's pension, letters from my Father's Lodge offering help and advice on the best way to apply for a place at the Masonic junior school at Weybridge, and documents covering claims for war damage.

Over the years, many people have asked me how I managed to get into the school. I had always known from Mother that she had to find Freemasons who were prepared to endorse my Petition. But until I looked over the contents of the tea chest, I was largely unaware of the great deal of time and effort she had devoted to the task.

While I was writing this account of my experiences at the Masonic schools, I not only recaptured many memories of childhood that inevitably had dimmed with the passing years, I also gained a better understanding of Masonic history and the remarkable story of how an Italian dentist, Bartolomeo Ruspini, conceived and put into action a plan to help the little girls of Freemasons who had fallen on hard times. And I have appreciated Mother's efforts to improve her lot in life all the more. Here was a woman who had enjoyed a comfortable lifestyle, suddenly reduced to near penury, with a child on the way. But for Father's decision to join the Masons, our existence would have been very bleak.

In the late 1920s, life for a single parent was far removed from what it is today. The Welfare State, now taken for granted, was still in its infancy. There was only minimal government support for someone in Mother's predicament. She had to find work, when the general assumption was that women did not work, and if they did they were expected to perform largely menial tasks. No anti–discrimination legislation then, no right to equal pay with men either. And all the while, there was the unfair social prejudice to cope with. Mother also lived through the war years. While I was relatively safe at school, she bravely stayed on to work in London's East End during the Blitz. Then in the evening, at her home in Worcester Park, she performed her duty as a Fire Warden. She faced unemployment both at the beginning and end of the war, yet despite adversity, carried on quietly, like so many other women of her generation. They never made a fuss, they simply got on with things.

My aim in writing this book was not only to record aspects of my life at Weybridge and Rickmansworth, but also to recognise my Mother's contribution and her desire to ensure that I had a better life than the one she had led. Going back over the past, made me appreciate once again the tremendous debt of gratitude I owe to all those Freemasons who supported both schools. They took to heart the Masonic ideal of caring for people less fortunate than themselves. This little book is my way of saying thank you.

With the passage of time, only the girls' school at Rickmansworth has survived. And it too has changed, reflecting the very different social climate of the last thirty years. It has been fee paying since the mid 1970s and is also open to girls whether or not their fathers were Freemasons.

In many ways, those few words I exchanged with my friend, summed up the mixed feelings I experienced during my school life. When I entered Weybridge in September 1936 for the first time, I knew I was only there because I had lost my Father. In letters home, I often looked forward to what I would be doing, 'This Time Next Week.' But ultimately, my friend was right of course. I had indeed been, "… one of the privileged few."

Barbara Kelland.

PART ONE

WIMBLEDON
1928

Kathleen always teased him about the length of time he spent in the bathroom every morning. Jimmy smiled to himself as he carefully shaved. He was being even more fastidious than usual, because later in the day he had to attend an important business meeting. He wanted to speak to his immediate boss about a turbo–alternator contract for the London Power Company.

He was so pleased to have found comfortable rooms to rent in Wimbledon. The landlady was a dear Miss Wilson 'Fleece,' whose snowy white hair had earnt her the nickname. Jimmy could hear his breakfast being prepared in the kitchen that looked out onto the long back garden. His little wife was a good cook and she always made sure the bacon was fried exactly the way he liked it. Nothing was too much trouble for her.

They had been married just over three years. During that time Jimmy had been based first in Norwich, then Poole and now he was back in London—which was so convenient because it was central to all the areas they both liked to visit. He could catch the train to Felixstowe, where he had once lived with his great friends Ruth and Dave Soames and for Kathleen it meant that she was nearer to her own family.

And it was also convenient for attending meetings at Jimmy's Masonic Lodge in Harwich, the 'Star in the East.' He had been a Freemason for many years, having been first introduced by his close friend Jack. Both men worked for the British Thompson Houston Company. Jack had inherited money from the family business and owned a large detached house with grounds and a tennis court in Rugby. (Later this was repossessed by the Ministry of Defence for Frank Whittle, the inventor of the jet engine). Jack was great to be around and Jimmy always had fun spending weekends with his friend's family.

While Jimmy was stationed in Norwich, enjoyable though those years were, he never seemed to have enough free time to visit Nancy, his elder sister, who lived in Plymouth. She was married with four children. He liked their company a great deal, and frequently got into heated political discussions with Dick, Nancy's husband. Oh how they argued! Dick a staunch socialist and Jimmy a Liberal supporter. Many a time he was asked to stand as a parliamentary candidate—only the request always seemed to come from the wrong party!

Now that Jimmy had been married for a few years, he realised the time had come to start thinking about providing for a place of his own—especially as in the New Year he would have additional responsibilities. He was absolutely delighted with Kathleen's news and wondered when they should tell Ruth and Dave. They had all planned to meet up during the coming weekend. He would ask Kathleen later that evening what she thought.

From the appetising aroma coming from the kitchen, Jimmy suddenly realised that breakfast was ready and he had better hurry or else he would be late.

Kathleen always liked to watch Jimmy go off to work. A jolly, happy man, he walked with a light step. That morning was no different. She waved him goodbye as he made his way along Rayleigh Road, stood a little longer than usual at the open door and then returned to the kitchen.

She too was delighted with the rooms they had found in Wimbledon. They were unfurnished and so for the first time in their marriage, she was free to choose the furniture for the home. The oak dresser was specially made from old wood and she loved the effect of the blue and white china dinner service arranged on its shelves. The living room was a good size. They had found an oak gate legged table and chairs to match and this provided a small eating area for their needs. She was so pleased to have persuaded Jimmy to buy the large palm, which really helped set off the small blue three piece suite.

Kathleen had quite a lot planned for the day ahead and busied herself in her little home. She was looking forward to the choir practice. She had a good soprano voice and was often given solo parts. Afterwards, she would meet Jimmy at her parents for a meal. The Methodists' Church on Waterloo Road was the centre for all the family's activities. It was here that she and Jimmy had got married and it was also where she sang in the choir. She was eagerly anticipating the evening as she made her way to Waterloo. The choir practice went very well and afterwards she was complimented on her singing. Kathleen said goodbye to her cousins and friends and hurried over to her parents' flat.

By now her mother and father were concerned that Jimmy had not arrived as arranged and it was getting late. Kathleen immediately began to fear the worst. Her husband was always so reliable and punctual. With a heavy heart she made the journey back to Wimbledon and Rayleigh Road. As she turned the corner she saw a policeman standing outside the house. Somehow Kathleen summoned the strength to continue.

"Tell me quickly, what has happened? Has he been injured?" she demanded, catching hold of the man by the arm.

The policeman replied calmly, "You must be very brave, it's much worse than that. Your husband is dead."

Kathleen's world crashed in around her.

In that instant, she realised that her good natured and big

hearted husband was gone forever. Her happy home in ruins. Their plans for a future together, no more. She suddenly felt very isolated, uncertain who she could turn to for comfort and support. She was twenty nine. Jimmy had celebrated his forty first birthday, just one month earlier. It was September 27, 1928 and Kathleen was already three months pregnant.

Only people who have had a similar experience to my Mother, will understand the devastating shock suffered when a loved one is taken away suddenly without warning. There was no kind policewoman to take her gently into the house and offer words of condolence and a cup of tea. Though I am sure Miss Lewis and the policeman did all they could to calm her down and steady her, before she made the return trip to her parents and brother at Waterloo.

It is impossible for me to imagine how she felt during that journey. Despite the passing years, she never fully recovered from the shock of my Father's death. In the late 1920s and early thirties, there was no real form of counselling for the bereaved, something Mother would have undoubtedly benefited from.

When she reached her parents' home, a telegram was waiting from the hospital. It said:

> Mr James Frederick Kelland had been found unconscious in Green Park and had been taken to Westminster Hospital, where he died between the hours of 7:30 pm and 8:30 pm on September 27. The cause of death was from a cerebral haemorrhage.

Her parents and brother were just as distraught as Mother. Frank went to the hospital to identify his brother–in–law. And then family and friends were notified and preparations made for the funeral. I am sure that the burden of all this was shared by the family, her aunt and cousins, who would have been willing to help out one way or another. The enormity of the event only fully sank in when the doctors informed Mother that had her husband survived, he would have been mentally incapacitated. It was the one last straw of comfort she could cling to. But it only offered temporary relief. For now she had another person to consider; her baby was due the following spring.

Outside the immediate family, there were three people Mother relied on to get her through the tough times; Ruth and Dave Soames, who my Father had regarded as his foster parents for the last twenty years, and Jack. It was to Jack that Mother turned for advice on how to approach Father's Lodge at Harwich. Jack was to prove a constant source of support whenever Mother needed him. He explained how she could ask for financial help and his advice was always good.

Father's funeral took place on October 3, 1928, and he was interred in Wimbledon Cemetery. Three weeks later the furniture from their little flat was put in a repository at the Elephant and Castle. It was then that Mother left London and went to stay with Ruth and Dave at Felixstowe to await my arrival. During this time Mother approached the 'Star in the East' Lodge for help and she received the generous amount of £1 a week until I was born. I am sure she appreciated this gesture and the money went to help with the extra expenditure that inevitably followed the birth of a new baby.

Mother's very personal loss had occurred eleven years before the start of World War II—an event that caused unimaginable turmoil on a scale never before witnessed. It also created many additional set backs for her. Yet she never gave up, always persevering, eager to improve her lot in life. And I was fortunate to benefit from her persistence in a very direct way.

MITRE STREET

1929–32

MITRE STREET, WATERLOO, APRIL 1929

After my birth on April 13, 1929 in Felixstowe, Mother returned to Waterloo sixteen days later. Grandfather was a caretaker for some flats in the area, and had obtained two rooms for us. These were opposite his own and were to be my home for the next four years. The rent was ten shillings a week and for that there was no bathroom, only a shared toilet and washing facilities on the landing!

My Mother was destitute. Father had died with no life insurance, no pension, little money in the bank and no property to inherit. There was no social security support for a single mother in 1929. Mother's only source of income was a weekly widow's pension of ten shillings and a child allowance of five shillings for me, until I reached fifteen. Faced with the stark reality of having to live on such a small amount of money, Mother realised she needed to find work quickly.

Her family was not well off. There was no one she could turn to for financial help. She would have to carry on as best she could by relying on her own efforts. My Mother may have been poor in the material sense, but she was rich in other ways. She was young, strong and healthy and possessed a great deal of determination. Coupled with these qualities she was very talented and skilled at sewing. The family had arrived in England in 1910–11 from the west coast of Ireland, where Grandfather had been in the coast guard service. Both my parents were born in Eire and Mother would return there in later years, when she needed to rest and recuperate.

With the help of his brother–in–law, Grandfather got a job as a caretaker in Waterloo, allowing the family to move to London. Mother had attended the local church school and then at the age of fourteen, together with her two cousins Ellen and Maisie, went to Bloomsbury Trade School, where she chose to study corset making.

It was not really very far to travel. In those days before the First World War, the buses were drawn by horses and I can hear Mother telling me it cost, "A ha'penny over the Bridge." That would have been from Waterloo Road across Waterloo Bridge to the Aldwich. Then the girls walked along Kingsway and on to Bloomsbury. Mother excelled at this craft and when she left school at the age of sixteen, she was soon employed and worked her way up to become in charge of a workroom. All the leading department stores had workrooms attached to them. In the early part of the last century, women had many of their clothes custom made, the men had bespoke tailoring for those who could afford it.

Otherwise there were shops such as the 50 Shilling Tailors and Burton's. In Oxford Street, there were many large privately owned department stores, like Marshall & Snellgrove and Fenwicks (in addition to the familiar big names that are still there today), and many smaller private businesses, which sadly have long since closed down.

Mother worked for a French woman who had a shop in Bond Street, which was always considered more 'up market' than Oxford Street! And she earned a good wage of between £3–4 a week, in the early 1920s. And so it was with all this wealth of real world experience, 'trade' as it was known, that she applied and

WIDOWS' ORPHANS' AND OLD AGE CONTRIBUTORY PENSIONS ACT, 1925.

Ref. No. 330 1/28

MEMORANDUM.

From
The INSPECTOR, MINISTRY OF HEALTH
(Insurance Department),
52, Broad Street,
Bloomsbury,
W.C. 2.

To

Mrs Kelland

1 4 - 1 0 1928.

Reference or Inquiry. | Reply.

1. With reference to your application under the above-mentioned Act, I propose to visit you on Tuesday, the 23rd inst. at about 1 o'clock, when you should have in readiness such of the following certificates as are in your possession or are available :—
 (a) Your husband's death certificate.
 (b) Your certificate of marriage.
 (c) The birth certificates of the children in respect of whom you have claimed children's allowances.

2. You should also have in readiness any documents or correspondence concerning your husband's National Insurance, e.g.,
 (i) Doctor's medical card.
 (ii) Record card showing what cards have been surrendered.
 (iii) Any health insurance cards or unemployment insurance books.
 (iv) Any letters from his Approved Society concerning his National Health Insurance.

3. If the date or time mentioned in paragraph 1 of this memorandum is not convenient please suggest hereon two alternative dates and times when it would be convenient for you to see me.

4. Any reply to this memorandum should be sent to me on this form as soon as practicable ; the form need not be stamped.

D. Franklin
for Inspector.

Form O.S.P. 13. (C.D.R.)
236 M154/5166 30/4/28 1,000 J.W.L.&O. 641

W.P. 211 (Revd.)
Please quote this number in all correspondence.

MEMORANDUM

1/690/Pel

From
THE CONTROLLER,
MINISTRY OF HEALTH,
INSURANCE DEPARTMENT,
BROMYARD AVENUE,
ACTON, LONDON, W.3.

To
Mrs Kelland

2 9 1936

Widows', Orphans' and Old Age Contributory Pensions Acts, 1925 to 1932.

In reply to your recent enquiry regarding further payment of allowance in respect of your child Barbara Joan an additional allowance for a child over the age of fourteen years is payable only if the child is under full-time instruction in a day school. The allowance continues so long as the child remains under full-time instruction in a day school, or to the 31st July next following the child's sixteenth birthday, whichever is the earlier.

An additional allowance is not, therefore, payable if your child attends a school. Your child is not disqualified by her entry into a Masonic School

W.P.107A.

Pen.
Claim No. K32426.
Please quote this number in all correspondence.

MEMORANDUM.

From
THE CONTROLLER,
INSURANCE DEPARTMENT,
MINISTRY OF HEALTH,
BROMYARD AVENUE,
ACTON, LONDON, W.3.

To
Mrs A. K. Kelland

15.5. 1929.

WIDOWS' ORPHANS' AND OLD AGE CONTRIBUTORY PENSIONS ACT, 1925.

The pension of 10/- a week payable to you under the above-named Act has been reviewed in consequence of the change of circumstances set out below, and a pension at the revised rate of 15/- a week has been awarded, subject to such adjustment as may be necessary in the event of further changes occurring.

You have already obtained payment of Pension Order(s) at the old rate for the period 16.4.29 to 30.4.29 and an underpayment of 15/- has therefore occurred. This has been adjusted by increasing the amount of pension payable for the week commencing , the date of the first Order in the new Pension Book.

The new pension order book can be obtained by completing the enclosed yellow form and presenting it at the Post Office mentioned.

Nature of Change of Circumstances :—

Birth of a posthumous child on 13.4.29.

ABOVE LEFT: the Inspector's notice to visit Mother. ABOVE: answer to Mother's enquiry, re the continuation of my allowance of five shillings: 'Your child is not disqualified by her entry into a Masonic school.' LEFT: confirmation of Mother's entitlement to a Widow's Pension.

was appointed to teach corsetery for two days a week on a part time contract at her old trade school in Bloomsbury—a name and place I was to become very familiar with.

Living next to her parents with her aunt nearby, Mother could leave me safely with them, even though I was just weeks old. This must have come as a great relief. There were no pre–school nurseries then and a nanny was unaffordable to say the least! This was a start and provided a very modest regular income, but she knew that she needed to find more. As Mother had worked in the West End, she still had many contacts there and managed to supplement her small pension and wage by taking in corset repair work, building up a private sewing practice on the strength of her earlier reputation.

Mother worked in the little living room, busy on the 'Singer' treadle machine. That machine earned our livelihood. The repair work was not very reliable of course and would fluctuate from week to week, depending on the number of corsets that needed repairing and more often than not altered.

Just everyday living was hard enough. The difference between what my Grandmother had to do in the home compared to today's housewife is so vast that if either of them could meet up again and change places, they would think they had landed on another planet. We take so much for granted. The young housewife expects all the electric appliances and conveniences that we have today as the norm not luxuries; luxuries that my Grandmother and Mother could not even have dreamt of.

Women's work was very physical, for all they had was a pair of hands that had to clean, wash, cook, bake, iron, sew, shop. Their strong arms and backs carried not only the daily shopping but the coal, which was needed to make fires to provide hot water and fuel for the range, on which they cooked. No microwaves, electric ovens, flick of the switch hot water systems, automatic washing machines or dishwashers for them. The beating, grating and whisking of food was all done by hand! The only fast food our family ate was fish and chips, which used to be cheap back then.

People wore clothes made from natural fibres, wool, cotton, linen and silk. The last two were expensive, the only kind of man made fibre available was rayon or artificial silk as it was known. With no central heating, double glazing or insulation, the rooms at Waterloo were cold. The only form of heating was from a range. It had an oven, hob and at the side a fire. It was this fire that kept the oven and hob hot and on which the women had to bake and cook and heat water for all the washing needs. Bathing was in a tin bath in front of the range, once a week. There was no power shower or bidet—that had to wait until the late 1960s before making an appearance in British homes.

Because of the poor heating, people wore many layers of clothes. The undergarments were made of wool. Flannel and flannelette night clothes and petticoats for the women, woollen combinations for the men and long woollen socks. Often these were hand knitted and because wool is soft it is easily worn into holes. So women had to be experts with a needle and darning mushroom.

As there was no television, it is easy to see how long evenings were passed in darning and mending. When cotton sheets became rather worn and thin in the centre, they were cut in two and the sides (where the selvedge edges were), would be joined in a single or better a double stitched flat seam down the middle. Narrow hems were made and machined on the sides of the sheet.

Children were dressed in clothes similar to the adults. Boys always wore short trousers, until they reached senior school age and both boys and girls wore leggings to keep themselves warm in the winter. These were usually made from leather and they were buttoned up along one side. They were shaped to fit over the top of the foot. The buttons were so close together, we used a special hook to fasten them. It was not uncommon for men to wear spats. These covered the tops of their shoes and ankles and

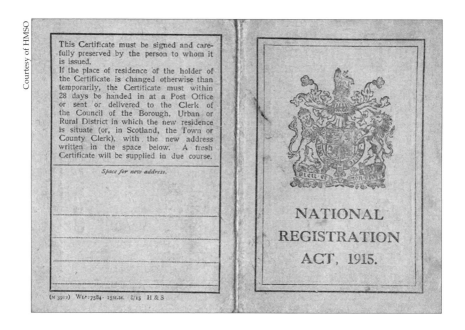

ABOVE and RIGHT:
Mother's certificate,
recording her trade as a
corset maker, which
entitled her to work in
the corset making
business. She was only
sixteen at the time.

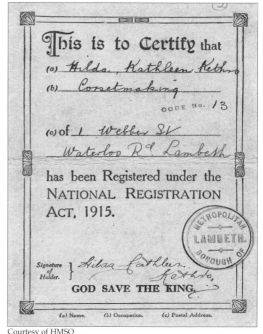

were also buttoned at the side. They were mostly worn for fashion. In the 1930s women still wore corsets, girdles and suspender belts. Tights were not introduced until the arrival of the miniskirt in the 1960s. Stockings were either made from silk, lisle (cotton) or wool. The fully fashioned stockings were shaped to fit the ankle and calf, there was a seam up the centre back and at the ankle, 'clocks,' which were delicate knitted patterns.

Stockings were held up with suspenders from a corset, girdle or suspender belt. All these clothes had to be carefully washed for there was no quick drying nylon and they were made from heavy woven cotton that did not stretch or lose its shape easily. Woollen garments were difficult to launder. They had to be carefully washed by hand with gentle soap flakes. 'Lux' was a particular brand I remember. Mother had long thin poles that she put through the sleeves of the garment with strong string at two ends and the centre of the clothes, and hung them on the washing line. Any woollens, including blankets were washed on a day when there was preferably a very strong wind. Money was never spent on sending clothes unnecessarily to the laundry or cleaners, quite simply there was no money left over for these things.

Grandfather had a shoe last made of iron, there were three feet of different sizes on it and because he was also skilled in the use of his hands, he could mend the family's shoes. The heels were often worn down very quickly because we walked everywhere. There was no car waiting outside the front door. We walked to the bus, tram (in London) or train station. To save money, we bought little metal curved pieces with spikes on one side called 'Blakeys,' and hammered these into the heel of our shoes, particularly if one side was already worn down.

I remember whenever Mother bought a new pair of shoes, she had 'Philips' rubber soles stuck on. This might seem an extraordinary step to take (sorry about the pun!), but it meant that the leather was preserved for longer and the shoe kept its shape, helped by the additional use of shoe trees.

It was no wonder that a tradition had grown up of having a roast dinner on Sunday and a cold meat dinner on Monday, since that was washday and what a day of labour it turned out to be for the woman running the house. There were clothes, bed linen and towels that had to be boiled and put in the bath on the range with soap powder. Other garments often required cleaning on the washboard, using a bar of 'Sunlight soap,' the water had soda added to 'soften it.' This kind of physical work was hard, rubbing the clothes up and down to remove the dirt.

To help dry things, Grandmother had a very large mangle. It seemed enormous to me. There were two wooden rollers and a handle on the right. The tension was controlled by a screw on the top. Under the rollers, was a large piece of wood, rather like a tray, at the front there was a space to let the water run through and we placed a bucket underneath. The clothes were held in the left hand between the wooden rollers and as the handle turned you had to be quick to move your fingers out of the way and make sure the bucket was correctly positioned, otherwise there would be water everywhere.

Many of the linens were washed with a squeeze of a 'blue bag' in the water. This was to help keep them white. Then they were dipped into starch. There was no spray on starch at the press of a nozzle, it had to be made. 'Robin' was the brand name, the powder was mixed into a smooth paste and boiling water added. The items for starching were then dipped through the solution. Ironed correctly on the right side, brought up a shine.

It was physically hard work lifting water laden clothes and household linen from the tin baths up to the mangle, then turning the handle. If the clothes were bulky this took a lot of energy. Once the washing had dried, the ironing began on Tuesday or later in the week. The irons that Mother and Grandmother used were of different weights and sizes. They were not electric or steam, and were known as flat irons—as if an iron was any other shape! My Grandmother used to heat an iron by placing it on the top of the range or gas hob. Before we could touch the hot handle, we needed little iron holders. These were circular and made of layers of woollen cloth, held together at the edge with a binding.

There was no dial to regulate the heat, we simply had to guess! The procedure used was as follows: we wetted two fingers and then very, very quickly, lightly touched the surface of the iron. If there was a sizzling sound then it was hot enough. Once, I even saw Mother carefully holding the iron to the side of her face, to gauge the exact heat.

Similarly, my Grandmother would open the oven door of the range, and put her hand in to test the temperature. And this woman baked everything from bread to roasts to cakes and pastries using guess work!

The curtains at the windows required cleaning frequently and Grandmother washed the net curtains every week. Living in the centre of London it was necessary. Each day was a battle against the soot and dirt. At this time, the capital still suffered with the thick green and yellow fog that used to engulf the city—pea soupers they were called, because it was often impossible to see a few yards in front of you.

The cooking ranges needed cleaning with black lead and special brushes were used for this purpose. These were oval in shape with a raised handle to keep your fingers as clean as possible. Black lead was applied, allowed to dry and then vigorously polished with another brush. We used Cardinal red polish on the quarry tiles by the range and again a similar polishing process. A lot of my Grandmother's cooking knives were not stainless steel. They were sharpened on a stone to give them an edge, but they tarnished easily and needed cleaning. This was done with a very fine emery paper, but before too long the blade became much smaller!

There were no refrigerators or freezers, so we had to buy food either weekly or daily in the case of perishables. Fortunately the shops and market stalls in the Cut and the Marsh were just a few yards from Mitre Street, so at least that meant no long journey to buy food. In those days it was cheap in London with market stalls everywhere, renowned for good value and bargains.

One of my strongest memories of these early years was the Muffin Man. I remember asking Mother for a penny, running down the stairs and along the pavement towards him. He balanced a large tray, filled with flat muffins on his head, and rang a handbell to let people know that he was in the street. He had one of those real old London cries, "Muffins! Muffins for sale!"

It was about this time in 1932, that Mother allowed me outside to play with the other children. Not long after my birth she had started a diary and wrote about the early years in Waterloo.

> There were no parks near enough and if there
> had been, children were not allowed onto the
> grass. So life was a very drab affair for the town
> child.

Hard as it is to believe today, there were still children running around the streets of London in bare feet and clothed in rags. Little girls and boys selling matches from trays, were not an uncommon sight.

My Grandmother and Great Aunt took it in turns to look after me while Mother was out to work. It must have taken all their patience to keep me amused and occupied in the small flat we lived in then. I do remember accompanying them both to the women's sewing circle at the Methodists' Chapel. This was held in one of the many rooms behind the Chapel, but I can only recall the image of seemingly never ending, dimly lit corridors, and to me they appeared so very wide. I am sure it became a problem to know what to do with me, as the streets were unsafe and there was nowhere for a child to play. I was growing older and within a few years would start formal schooling.

During the early part of the 1930s, London began to expand into the surrounding counties. New homes were being built in the suburbs and people were leaving London to start new lives away from the dirt and thick fog that was part of winter life in the capital. So it was not very surprising that Mother was thinking along these lines and planning a move of her own.

WORCESTER PARK
1933–36

WORCESTER PARK, 1933

During the summer of 1932, Mother decided she would try to leave London and find a place to live in Surrey. The expanding suburbs of the capital were creating a great inter war house building boom.

In September 1932, she wrote in her diary:

> We had no sooner returned (from holiday) when Nannie and I went to look at the little house on Stoneleigh Avenue, Worcester Park and decided to take it. We are now awaiting one to be built like it and then we hope to move in the New Year.

By January 20, 1933, the house was ready and Mother and Grandparents prepared to leave London. I knew Mother had somehow managed to save the £30 deposit required and that the corner house was too expensive, so we had one in the middle of the terrace. She had also taken into account that there was only a front and back to maintain, no extra guttering and roof to look after and repair. The wooden windows and doors were painted brown, not the black and white she would have liked, because

Tele: Streatham 3121 (3 lines)

33, Streatham Place,

Brixton Hill,

LONDON, S.W.2.

Dear Sir or Madam,

Re. Stoneleigh Park Estate,
Worcester Park.

We have pleasure to place before you particulars of the soundest property investment yet made, and we feel sure that if you are considering house purchase you will take an early advantage to call to the estate office which is situate in Stoneleigh Drive, 3 minutes only from Worcester Park Station (Southern Railway) via any London terminus and Wimbledon - or direct Waterloo line and Clapham Junction. Upon leaving the Station at Worcester Park turn left, and Stoneleigh Drive is the first turning on the right.

These properties which have an 18 ft. frontage and 27 ft 3" depth with large gardens front and back are saleable at £525 freehold which price includes all legal and Conveyance fees-Road and paving charges - electric light to lampholders, gas fire and cooker points, hot and cold water throughout from boiler - panelled bath and pedestal basin, in fact no extra charges whatever. Corner Houses are £535: £40 deposit, same mortgage terms.

The total all-in deposit is £30 and the weekly repayments are 16/8d. The district rate is 8/-d in the £ per annum and the rates will be approximately 3/-d per week upon £20 assessment or 19/8d per week inclusive.

The accommodation of these houses will be three bedrooms, two reception rooms, W.C. and bathroom, Kitchen and Hall decorated to your choice at limited cost, very spacious we assure you.

The return rail fares from Worcester Park Station are as follows:-

		£. s. d.		£. s. d.
Waterloo	1 week 3rd	7. 9	Bank	8 0
	1 month "	1. 7. 6	"	1. 9. 0
	3 " "	3.13. 3	"	3.19. 0
Vauxhall	Quarterly 3rd Class	......£3. 5. 0		
Clapham Junction	" " "	......£2.15. 0		
Wimbledon	" " "	......£1.14. 9		

ABOVE: the particulars of Mother's new house in Worcester Park, built by John Cronk & Sons.
LEFT: the receipt for the deposit.

that would have been cheaper when the house required repainting. All these points she would have considered. What did they all think about the move? Here are Mother's own words:

> January 20, 1933.
> Today we moved from Mitre Street, London, to Worcester Park. What a day we had! I had our Tibby cat in a basket and the little dear tried to get out and rubbed his nose raw. I had Grandpa, Nannie you and the cat to look after. My word, wasn't the road in a mess. It had been raining and there was mud everywhere. We had only just arrived at the house, when the van with our furniture turned up. There was a grand rush to get the things in before dark, because the electric light meter was not fixed. So all we had was a candle to see with. We managed to get the beds up and were all thankful when it was time to go to bed that night. Tibby we put into the bathroom 'till he became more used to the new place. Each time he wanted to go out, I always put him on a lead. You see, I was so afraid I would lose him, he was such a dear pet, he belonged to your Daddy. The front and back gardens were one mass of mud and clay and a garden seemed hopeless.

One thing still has not changed, the stress of moving house is the same now as it was back then in the 1930s. By March 12, 1933, Mother wrote:

> We began to lay the path in the garden and ten weeks from then we had flowers blooming in the beds. I can call it a garden now, for indeed it

is growing in every direction. Grandpa has the kitchen garden planted and we have rather a pretty flower patch with a lawn. We hope to do plenty of sunbathing there during the summer.

Mother helped with a lot of the physical work, laying the lawn and paths and making a rockery. She could not afford all the stones, so she made some from cement. This rockery was at the end of the house, outside the French windows. Mother liked to tell the story of when she went to order the turf at the coal merchant's 'Parkers,' next to the railway station. Having been brought up on the west coast of Ireland, she was used to calling turf 'sods,' so you can imagine the reception she received and the look on the men's faces when she ordered all the sods for the garden! Stoneleigh Avenue was now our little home. The contrast

March 1933: the back garden at Worcester Park starts to take shape after a lot of hard work.

of the Surrey fields to the rooms in London, must have been very marked indeed. Grandfather could grow vegetables again as he had done when he was living as a coast guard in Ireland. I remember him sitting outside the little shed, smoking his pipe and looking every inch like the sailor on the 'Players' cigarette packet and for that matter, to my young eyes at least, so did King George V!

The garden had eating and cooking apple trees, logan berries, gooseberries and black current bushes and plenty of space for all the onions, carrots and cabbages.

Grandmother now had a small kitchen with hot and cold water and a stone sink with a wooden draining board. There was a coke fuelled boiler to provide the hot water, and next to it was just enough space for a gas cooker. No more cooking on a range, no more black leading to do either.

On the other side of the kitchen close to the back door, was a very large cupboard. Grandfather had been able to cut away the lower part so that the large mangle could fit underneath it and next to that was a kitchen cabinet. Here all the dried food stuffs were kept in the top cupboards and in the centre was a pull out table, it was on this surface that Grandmother did the baking and pastry rolling. No more using the deal top table, which in the past had doubled as a dining table and required scrubbing each time.

My Grandparents had the use of the two ground floor rooms. Their bedroom was in the front and the dining room in the back, where we ate our meals together. Grandmother still cooked for the four of us.

Mother and I had the two bedrooms upstairs. The one in the front became our living room and had a bow window. Mother placed the 'Singer' treadle machine in here. I used to sleep beside Mother in the double bed in the other bedroom.

To have a bathroom with all the proper facilities must have been marvellous for everyone. No more sharing of communal washing facilities. No more toilet on the landing. The boiler was only put on for hot water, for bathing at the weekends and washday, which was always a Monday. The rest of the time we heated water in a kettle and brought it upstairs. There was no money to have the boiler on continuously, but I doubt whether the adults would have found this a hardship, because they were now in their own little home. The third bedroom at the front of the house over the hall, was very small. There was just enough space for a bed or in our case an ottoman. This was like a couch with one end raised and covered in fabric. The 'sitting' area opened up and became invaluable storage for all Mother's fabrics. I had a little cupboard in the corner which I used as my little playroom and where I kept my childhood 'treasures.'

All the main rooms contained fireplaces, with tile surrounds and mantle pieces. Level with the top of the doors were picture rails on every wall. It was standard to have a central electric light in each room but I cannot recall any sockets. This may sound very strange to us today, only there were no mass produced domestic appliances, not even a basic refrigerator or telephone.

Perishable goods were bought daily, though fortunately the milk was delivered to the door. Keeping the food fresh was a challenge. There were porous terracotta pots, which when wet were supposed to help keep the milk cool if placed over the bottle. Otherwise in hot weather, milk was boiled every evening so that it had cooled by breakfast time. Butter was kept by placing its dish in contact with cold water. Part of the large cupboard was used as a larder and had air holes in the rear wall.

Worcester Park Central Road had a very good range of shops. I remember 'David Gregg the Grocer,' where the butter was on display in very large blocks behind a glass screen, labelled with its country of origin—it was not bought ready packaged. The shop assistant curled off the amount of butter ordered, put it on a piece of greaseproof paper on the scales and when the required weight was reached, slapped the butter into a rectangle using wooden pats, shaped like ridged paddles with short handles.

Biscuits were not packaged either. In front of the counter at 'David Gregg's,' there were containers with glass on one side, so we could see the loose biscuits and buy just the amount we required. As you can imagine, a lot of the biscuits got broken. These were a very good buy because although they were all mixed varieties, they were always very cheap and useful in recipes. You could buy all your everyday needs in the shops in

Worcester Park, Central Road in the 1930s.

Central Road, but now instead of an easy walk back from the Cut and the Marsh, Grandmother had to carry shopping up the hill. This was a walk and steady climb taking between fifteen and twenty minutes. I am sure that on some days she must have found it very hard.

There was no public transport to take people around the estates. Some of the houses had small garages. And there was a cinder covered pathway between the terraces and along the backs of the gardens. Two of our immediate neighbours did have cars, but I do not recall any other vehicles near our house. I had to wait until 1947 before I got the chance of actually being driven in a car. Today it hardly seems possible that we used to walk to the shops, walk to the station at Worcester Park, walk to the Central Road to catch a bus to Cheam or Sutton.

Our house was near the top of a hill and we could go either way to the station. Down to Worcester Park or up the hill a little and then down to Stoneleigh station. If I walked further on to the end of Stoneleigh Park Road, I could catch a bus to Ewell, Epsom or Kingston. It was from here that I got on the 'Green Line' buses, which went to what seemed to me, far off places in Surrey and beyond.

Grandmother now had a garden, where she could hang out the laundry on a line supported with a prop. This was always taken down once the washing was finished, together with the big wooden post to which the rope was secured, leaving the garden uncluttered. Today I have a rotary line, but I still dismantle it when the clothes are dry. I do not like washing lines in the garden either!

There were trees at the back of the house. These were on the railway embankment, the actual tracks being down a very steep embankment. This was the local line to Waterloo, or to Epsom and further south in Surrey. Although the trains were so close, we became accustomed to the noise, which eventually was not very intrusive. The goods trains would pass during the night. Being the poor sleeper that I was and still am, I would often hear the clank clank of the buffers as the trains came to a halt.

Although we played along the back of the gardens and down the cinder track, I knew never to climb through the wires and onto the embankment. This was regarded as dangerous and it was also trespassing. Besides, I also thought it very frightening.

Just a few hundred yards away from our house was a brick field, which we approached through one of the sidings and over a small bridge. There was a tall chimney but for us as small children, it was out of bounds. In these early days, there were still green fields on the other side of the railway and young though I was, I have never forgotten seeing sheep grazing nearby.

A road away from Stoneleigh Avenue, was a large recreation ground with grass, somewhere at last for children to play! This was one of the routes to the new school that had been built near Sparrow Farm Road. From Mother's diary:

> You have begun school again but not at the one where you commenced your school days, a beautiful new school has been built almost on this estate. You do enjoy yourself, school does

not seem to worry you, for which I am very glad.

Mother supplemented her part time teaching by doing repair work and in July 1935 she wrote:

> I am going to Switzerland. For some months now I have been working for a surgical firm of corset making and I have made rather a lot of money and as the chance has come along I am going.

This holiday was organised through the Bloomsbury Trade School and I know that she enjoyed the experience and had so much to tell me. When she returned, Mother received notification from Head Office—her name for where the administration of the Masonic schools was organised in Great Queen Street, London.

> Oh what lovely news we have received! I have heard from Head Office and the Masons are granting me £25 per year for your education to begin as from September 1935, 'till you enter the junior boarding school at Weybridge. Isn't that just too good?

> September 4, 1935.
> You have begun school again after the summer holidays. This week I am going to arrange your transfer to the Kingsley High School, which you will attend on September 18, so you can make a good start with the other new students.

> All arrangements are now complete. Mr C is to become your guardian re your education whilst

we wait 'till you leave home. We have had a nice cheque to buy all your new uniform. It is very smart. The usual gym slip, white blouse, navy blue and white tie, white socks and black shoes, blazer with a lovely white badge. Panamas with navy and white badge and band, also a light blue frock with collar and cuffs in white. In the winter a velour hat and for wet days a navy bonnet, black stockings, big refer coat and a navy mac, also a scarlet jersey. You are having dancing lessons after school each Wednesday and you wear a scarlet dance frock, dancing shoes and scarlet tap shoes.

Later in life, whenever I thought about my early childhood days, I could always recall having sometime owned a little scarlet dress. It was not until I read Mother's diary many years later that I realised the little dress was the one worn at Kingsley High School for dancing.

From Mother's diary, September 18, 1935:

I have just returned from taking you to your new school. It's a lovely big private house in The Avenue. You attend school at 9:30 am, lunch from 12:00 pm 'till 2:15 pm and finish at 4:00 pm. On arriving home today, you are delighted with the new school and I feel sure you will be very happy.

October 15, 1935.
You have brought home a blue ticket which means ten marks for learning all your tables. The teacher is very pleased with you.

November 15, 1935.
Ten marks for drill. You certainly are taking after me in that subject.

The Turog Bread Co are launching a competition amongst the schools of England to colour a printed design which they have prepared. It must be done at school. Your teacher has sent up your effort along with ten others.

You could not get home quickly enough to tell me that the Headmistress called you out before all the school in the hall and you began to get panicky as you wondered what you had done. Miss Newman said the school was going to be very proud of one of the babies, as Barbara Kelland was the only child to win a prize of two shillings and six pence.

It was all over England and 5,000 children entered for sixty nine prizes. So we consider you a very good little girl to get even a consolation prize.

Strange how parts of this incident have remained in my mind. I can remember having to stand up in front of all the other children and feeling rather nervous, after all I was still only six years old. But I do not really recall the reason why!

Mother only took me to school on my first day, afterwards I had to walk there and back home by myself. This was nothing new for me. Since starting school at the age of five, I had walked with the other children from Stoneleigh Avenue. I remember distinctly a group of us going across the recreation ground from the new school in Sparrow Farm Road. Kingsley High was further away from our house, and as the only child attending it from our area, I was often walking on my own. There were several roads I had to cross. Apparently I had been observed by one of the mothers who lived near us. Mother was approached to see if she would allow me to escort the other little girl to school and so it was that I did not have to walk by myself anymore.

If Mother had fetched me back and forth from Kingsley High twice a day, she would have been forced to stop her own work. I had to learn to be sensible and go on my own. I was used to walking about by myself. On the days when Mother went to London to teach, I used to go down to the end of Stoneleigh Avenue and then Linwood Drive to the corner of Central Road and there I would wait for her to come from the station.

I did not have many of the material things of today's young children, but I had a degree of freedom at a very early age that they may probably not experience to the same extent.

Back in the 1930s, you communicated with people by either writing letters or sending a post card. If you needed to get a message to someone quickly, you used a telegram, as Father had done in 1924, telling Mother the time he was arriving home from a business trip. There were no faxes, no emails and very, very few people had telephones. Certainly no member of our immediate family had one and of course, mobile phones had yet to be invented. Writing to people was time consuming and then you had to

A telegram, sent by Father in 1924, telling Mother the time he was arriving home.

wait for them to reply. Those periods of waiting must have added to the strain and tension Mother would have undoubtedly experienced, uncertain about the final outcome of her Petition to the Masons for my place at Weybridge.

At the beginning of 1936, I had returned to Kingsley High School. Mother wrote:

> January, 1936.
> You have been put up into the Upper Form and are the youngest. I am really sorry, as I feel they are pushing you forward too quickly. You are not used to dictation and as you did not know how to spell the words you thought that you would guess them. On looking through your book (you do homework), I came across 'dusy.' After a lot of pulling it to pieces and a few questions to you, I find it is supposed to be 'does he.' YOU should be in the Upper Form?

I had also started to learn French and Mother says that I seemed to be getting on quite well. And what lesson have I remembered after all these years? Yes, the French lesson. I can vaguely recall the position of the door and the windows, going to open and close them and obviously I enjoyed this active approach. Oh, how I wished during the following years we had started to speak French at Weybridge! It has always been a mystery to me why we did not, and my goodness what a help that would have been when I went to Rickmansworth. Mother's diary continued:

> At the end of the term you had a party at school and a fancy dress competition. You went in your Mickey Mouse costume and won first prize, which was a huge shock. You also went to

several parties and wore the beautiful georgette frock that Miss Leach, who taught at Bloomsbury, had given you the previous Christmas. Apparently it caused a lot of comment from some of the ladies present.

Your school report is very good indeed. It has been sent to Head Office, so if they return it I will put it in this diary for you. (But it never was returned).

January 1936, saw the death of King George V. This is the account that Mother, a monarchist, wrote in her diary:

I must record for you in my diary the death of our King George V. He has only been ill four days and we cannot yet grasp the fact that he is no longer with us.

I have attended the lying in state of our late King George. I was one of the many thousands who lined up and formed a queue, miles long and thirty people deep. At 2:45 pm it was then on the Vauxhall side of the river and right down near Lambeth Bridge. We passed the other side of the bridge at night near 8:00 pm and marched past the Bier in the hall at 9:45 pm. I shall never forget it.

I caught the 5:23 am train from Worcester Park and went to London. Walked into St James' Park and paid sixpence for a chair. There I sat 'till the funeral came along just after 10:00 am. I could not have had a better view if I had paid pounds.

I wished afterwards I had taken you with me for there was plenty of room and you could have easily seen all the Kings and Princes and our Princesses. I was in the front row of chairs.

I knew that George V was our King. At Christmas we had all gathered at Uncle Frank's house around the wireless (as the radio was called) to hear his Christmas message. During the broadcast, the King's voice became a little croaky. Uncle Frank's mother–in–law said, "Cough man, cough," and the King obligingly did as he was told, where upon we all laughed and always remembered that Christmas message.

The family was still very much in touch with each other. Mother and Uncle Frank had moved out of London and they had both bought houses in Worcester Park and Stoneleigh. Grandmother's sister had remained at Waterloo and her daughters and their husbands were also nearby. We still visited Nellie and Maisie and because there were no other children in the family, I was still an only child surrounded by adults. When they met up together, I was always given something with which to occupy myself.

The time I enjoyed best was visiting cousin Maisie. She had boxes of jewellery and a seemingly unending number of small tables, stools and a trolley on which I used to set out all the items. The adults pacified me eventually, by buying from my little jewellery store. Although I was absorbed to a certain extent in my task of arranging all the pieces, I was bound to pick up some of the things the adults talked about.

I knew that in 1935 the Italians had invaded a country called Abyssinia and that the country's leader was someone called Haile Selassie. I had started a little stamp collection and was always looking out for additions to my album. Mother and I had found a stamp shop near the old post office in Worcester Park. I can still recall her pointing out this rectangular shaped stamp, so unlike our own and saying to me that the man whose picture was on the front, had been forced to leave his country and that there would never be any more stamps displaying his image ever again. So naturally I was very pleased to have the Abyssinian stamp in my collection.

I knew that the Prince of Wales had been proclaimed King and that there was unrest in the country, though I did not understand why. I remember Mother was rather shocked at hearing that someone she knew, was a supporter of the British Fascist leader Oswald Mosley, who marched around the streets of East London in a brown shirt.

Mother had always saved a portion of her income. She realised it was necessary to put something aside, not only for emergencies but for holidays too. During the break in the school year whilst teaching at Bloomsbury, she would also have benefited, because she could take in extra repair and alteration work. She also tried to see that for my birthdays and at Christmas there were special treats.

On these occasions from the time I was a baby, I had been showered with gifts not only from family members, but from kindly people who knew of Mother's circumstances. Not rich themselves, they nevertheless managed to find that extra little gift for me.

We did not go on holiday every year—Mother could not afford it, but when we did, it was always to friends. We were fortunate in knowing people who lived at three seaside resorts, Felixstowe, Southsea and Plymouth.

Because we had not visited anybody at Easter in 1936, Mother had saved enough money for a treat in the summer. This was going to be a special holiday that I would not forget in a hurry. Mother had planned a four week trip to Ireland. We were to stay with her childhood friend. The two women had communicated with each other ever since Mother had left. I think she was very excited at the prospect of going back and meeting Maggie Ellen again after a twenty four year break. This is Mother's account of how the journey started:

> What excitement there is to be sure! Cases all packed. Tickets bought. First Class saloon births on the ship. Ready for our Irish holiday.

Three months passed before Mother made another entry in her diary:

> I have only just found time to write about our holiday. The mad rush through the night by train to Wales. Waking you up and going on board the boat and how just outside Hollyhead the boat gave such a big role, you squeezed my arm and said you were falling. I kept saying if you didn't lie still you would be sick. After a lot of tossing you got off to sleep and then it took me quite a time to wake you at 5:30 am. We were then just running into Dun Laoghaire harbour. At long last we were on Irish soil and soon, so soon, I should see that dear childhood friend who I had written to for all those years, and with whom we were going to stay. We travelled all day and did not meet my friend 'till 9:30 pm that night. Still it was good and we enjoyed the journey. I'm sure you remember it and we have all the snaps.

> You ran as free as the air and as wild as the rabbits, enjoying the lonely stretches of strands and looking for baby crabs amongst the rocks and now the sad time was coming. We were on

the way to England again. You had said
goodbye to all your Irish friends and the day for
the Weybridge School was drawing near.

What a good reason for taking me far away to the west of
Ireland so that I would not even think about what lay ahead for
me. I can recall parts of that journey and the holiday as well. I
remember the sleeping quarters on board ship. We did not have a
separate cabin, and it seemed to me that the two tier births were
in a large open area. I sat up when the boat started to roll and
Mother told me to lie down and suck a barley sugar.

Mother was the most incredibly good sailor, never sea sick. In
future years, she would often make the trip over to Dublin. After
one particularly rough crossing, she was the only person, along
with the captain, left standing and capable of walking off the ship
unaided.

When we eventually got to Dublin, it was time for an early
lunch. I should have regarded this as a special treat, for it was
fresh Irish salmon, but I did not like it at all—I was used to eating
salmon from a tin and the parsley sauce was not to my taste
either! It would be many years before I had fresh salmon again.

Part of the journey was by train. I found myself sitting on a
very hard wooden seat, or so it seemed to me and the train that I
thought was very slow, was powered by peat.

The final part of our journey was by coach. I sat by the window
holding a china doll that Mother had beautifully dressed and
which was the centre of much interest when we stopped at small
villages on our way to county Mayo. The doll was not mine but a
present for Maggie Ellen's eldest daughter Mary, who was just
one year younger than me. Mother had a suitcase and so did I.
Not only did mine contain my few holiday clothes, but it was full
of all the garments I had grown out of—these were all for Maggie
Ellen's family. Years later, Mary told me how delighted she was to
have been first in the family to wear these clothes from England.

There are memories of riding bare back on a donkey that was hell bent on charging off towards the peat bogs, or so I thought. I remember hanging on to its mane for dear life and I never wanted to go near a creature like that again and never have! There were lobsters, fresh from the Atlantic and oh dear, I did not like watching them being cooked. It was whilst staying at this home that I squashed my left thumb in the very strong back door. I was on my way to the outside toilet and I can remember Mother telling me to be careful as there was a strong wind blowing and while trying to heed her advice, I shut the door on my thumb. I should think my screams were heard in Dublin! The poor thumb has remained a different shape all my life.

We spent some of the time in Blacksod. This was Maggie Ellen's childhood home, where the two girls had gone to the local school, walking the three miles together and along the way exchanging their packed lunches. Mother liked the Irish bread baked by Maggie Ellen's mother and Maggie liked the English bread baked by my Grandmother, (who had lived in Blacksod while Grandfather was stationed there in the coast guards). Maggie's family home where we stayed, was just the width of a narrow road away from the Atlantic Ocean. I thought it was wonderful going to sleep in the evening, listening to the sounds of waves crashing onto the beach.

In August, we returned to England, back to face the biggest challenge of my life. And so September drew near.

The long years of waiting and wondering for Mother were coming to an end. Just because she was the widow of a Freemason with a daughter, did not automatically entitle her to send me to the Masonic Girls' School at Weybridge. From the time I was three years old, Mother had been in contact with Father's Lodge, the 'Star in the East.'

The conditions for acceptance were strict and the time involved very drawn out, so it was important for Mother to begin the application procedure several years before I reached my seventh birthday. (This was the earliest age for a child to be admitted into the school).

She was helped to a great extent by the secretary of Father's Lodge and I am sure by Jack, who would have been anxious to see his Goddaughter accepted into the Girls' School. As he was a Mason, he would have known about the philanthropic ideals and the tremendously high standards that were demanded by the Freemasons.

The Secretary of the 'Star in the East' Lodge, told Mother she had to apply for a Petition to be answered, which was sent with certificates of marriage, birth and death to the General Committee. In 1934, Mother had written in her diary:

> I have to go back a little bit in time. Your Daddy was a Freemason and I had made up my mind that when you were old enough, I should endeavour to get you into the Masonic School, where the education is the best in the land.

> Since you were three years of age, I have written and kept in touch with the Lodge and now that you are reaching six I have written again. In reply, I have had a Petition form to fill in and have paid a few calls at your school. The Headmaster told me I was doing a wise thing

and that I should never regret it. There has been
no end of writing to do over this and a lot of
running about to get Masons to sign etc. A Mr C,
who I knew years ago in London lives here and
he is going to help me all he can.

The entry procedure into the Royal Masonic Institution for
Girls was very strict. Freemasons' widows who wanted their
children to be considered, had to comply with certain criteria. I
know Mother had to have the support of several Masons who
were prepared to endorse her application. The procedures were
lengthy and thorough. By the spring of 1935, Mother wrote in her
diary:

I have heard from the Masons and the Petition
has gone through, so now we have to await
events.

My Petition was finally approved in May 1935, and my name
recommended to the General Court for placement on the list of
candidates for election to the junior school. By July 12, Mother
received notification I had been unanimously elected without a
ballot and as a result I received a grant for out–education from
October until such time as I could be admitted. The most likely
date being set for September 1936. It must have come as a great
relief to know that after all the years of writing and tracking down
contacts, Mother's persistence had finally paid off. I said earlier
she had many fine qualities and determination was certainly one
of them.

The school where I was out–educated had to meet with the
approval of the General Court and a Freemason was appointed as
an Almoner, who was charged with the administration of my
grant, and supervised my case. Everything was carried out in
strict compliance with the rules set out in the documents that

Mother received, otherwise I could not be admitted. She had to find a Freemason who was willing to be the Almoner and oversee all the arrangements, obtain the names and addresses of Mother's proposed guarantors and also the details of the two friends who would act as referees.

It was now that the connection with the Methodist Chapel at Waterloo played a part. For Mr C, who supervised everything was known to Mother from her time living at Waterloo. He was well placed to help her with all the paperwork.

I also had to pass a little examination in reading, writing and at least one of the first four rules of arithmetic. This test was carried out under the supervision of a certified school mistress, Miss Newman, the Headmistress of Kingsley High School, whom I remember as a kind woman, and I am sure she was pleased to have overseen this. Revaccination was required and Mother had to obtain special permission to have this done earlier that August 1936, because she had planned for the special holiday in Ireland.

Mother had not only been busy with all the forms to fill in from the Masons, but she was also concerned about her state widow's pension and whether this would be affected by my attending the Masonic School. Fortunately there was no change in her entitlement, bringing much relief I am sure.

On the day I was received into the Junior School at Weybridge, I first had to undergo a medical examination and if all went well, I would be admitted on, 'Tuesday the 15th September, at 2:30 pm precisely.'

WEYBRIDGE
1936–39

WEYBRIDGE, SEPTEMBER 1936

It was a warm September day when I put on my clothes, in preparation for my journey to Weybridge. My Aunty Annie had knitted me a little outfit for the big day. She had helped to look after me when I was a baby and a little one, taking turns with my Grandmother, while my Mother went out to work.

Her two rooms in Mitre Street looked out onto the side of the Old Vic Theatre. I would sit on the window seat while she knitted, long needles tucked under her armpits, combing and brushing her hair. She was the only family member who allowed me to do that! I would plait and then coil it around the side of her head.

The little outfit was knitted in an eau–de–Nil green and white, Mother's favourite colours. It consisted of a skirt, where the panels of alternate plain and purl gave the effect of pleats, a little green and white striped jumper and a green cardigan with a white stripe at the cuffs. What length socks I wore and the type of shoe, I have no recollection. Neither do I recall the train journey or the walk from Weybridge station to the school.

I only remember sitting in the Common Room, on the left hand side near the end. All the adults were seated on chairs, while the little girls admitted that day, sat on stools in front of their mothers or closest relative. Across the room immediately opposite Mother and me, was a girl rocking back and forth on her stool, looking very unconcerned, as she took in her surroundings. Behind her, a very sad gentleman. I can vaguely recall him, but it was Mother who remembered how downcast he looked.

The little girl's name was Jacqueline (Jackie) and the sad gentleman, her Grandfather. They had come all the way down from Sunderland. Jackie and I would end up in Dormitory Four and be in Zetland House together when we joined the senior school at Rickmansworth. Both septuagenarians now, ever since that first September day in 1936, we have remained in contact.

"Come and see where I'm going to sleep! Come and see where I'm going to sleep!" I called back to Mother as I skipped in front of her along the brown linoleum covered corridor that led from Dormitory Three, passed the stairs, down to the kitchen and to Dormitory Four, directly opposite the Headmistress's study.

A picture of me, taken by Mother in front of the old school wing. The lower bay window was the dining room, the first floor bay window Dormitory Four and the single window to the left of it, the pupil teacher's bedroom.

It was a strange layout really. There were two fireplaces at an angle to each other opposite the door. One faced a small room containing three beds and French doors leading out onto a small wooden veranda. The other fireplace faced a large room with six beds and a lovely bay window that overlooked the main garden. It was wide and sweeping, so we had this lovely vista of green grass. There was a tall poplar tree in the left hand corner and in the centre a beautiful rose arch, behind which was a vegetable garden.

Jackie was Number 26 and in the middle bed of the smaller room. I was Number 30 and in the second bed on the larger side of the dormitory. There was a dressing table with a mirror in the bay window. The beds were covered with counterpanes, which I expect were white, with flower borders and beside every bed was a chair.

Mother must have prepared me very well for my new life and the fact that I was to leave her and my home at the age of seven years. I was not in the least bit worried or upset. Mother was the one who had cause for concern.

During the afternoon, each girl was called out to have a medical examination. When I was born, the left side of my body was squashed. From my nose that lay flat on my face, to my left ribs that stuck out and my spine and neck, which I could never hold completely straight. The dear midwife had massaged my little nose back into its correct position, as she knew Mother's circumstances and did not want her to see a deformed baby. Mother feared that even at this late stage I could still be rejected. However, luckily all was well and I passed my medical.

Later the same afternoon, older girls appeared at the Common Room doorway. I can recall two of them very clearly. One was quite pretty, with fair wavy hair, the other girl taller with straight black hair and rather serious expression. I just knew who would be my 'House Mother' and my heart sank. And naturally, I was right. Barbara F looked after Bettina, who was also a new girl that day and was two years older than me. Avril, the dark haired girl, looked after me. I do not think my pairing was very successful, since I was so much younger and was overwhelmed by my strange surroundings, taking longer to settle in than Bettina. Barbara and Avril were nearly eleven years old and would soon move to the senior school at Rickmansworth. Perhaps when the older girls had come to look after us and show us around the school, our mothers departed, for there were no tearful farewells.

The other big event I recall from that first day was bedtime. I had taken my own clothes off, down as far as my vest, and from this garment I would not be parted! Later in the evening, a young Matron was on duty, a Miss Iris Wade (who was to become Head Matron of Rickmansworth).

"What's your name?" she said to me, standing at the bottom of my bed.

"Barbara Kelland," I replied.

"Oh Kelly baby," she said and that was it.

Kelly I became and Kelly I remain to this day to all the girls I grew up with. And yes Miss Wade did manage to part me from the vest! My home clothes were taken away and I did not see them again until December. The final memory I have of starting at Weybridge school was my first morning. After going to the bathroom, it was back to the dormitory to dress before a bell rang to tell us it was time to kneel beside our beds and say our prayers.

I was sitting on top of my bed. Laid out before me, was the strangest looking piece of clothing I had ever seen. It appeared to have openings, buttons and arms in every conceivable place. I sat and turned it around. First one way, then another. No, I still could not get it right. I tried again, getting in more and more of a muddle. It was at that moment when Barbara F, in the bed next to mine, came to my aid. She positioned the garment correctly and showed me how to put it on. The article of clothing in question was a pair of combinations. I was to become very familiar with this scratchy uncomfortable garment, for many years to come.

W hat was it about Weybridge that so appealed to us as little children? For appeal it certainly did. Many decades later at an Old Girls' reunion day in June, Mary, Margaret, Pat and myself were sitting at one end of a large refectory table in the Dining Hall at tea time, reminiscing about our years at Weybridge. We all spoke of the good times there with a great deal of affection, unlike our first experiences at the much larger Masonic school at Rickmansworth.

Weybridge always reminded me of a typical large Surrey house. There were two parts to the school. The old wing consisting of dormitories, classrooms, a quiet room, shoe, cloak and old drill rooms, the dining room, kitchen, staff dining room and the Head Matron's and Headmistress's studies and the main school entrance.

The new wing was an extension. Even as a child I did not like it. I found it oddly impersonal. I preferred the old wing with the vine and wisteria growing up the walls, the little wooden veranda and the leaded bay windows. The main Common Room was in the new wing. This was where we always assembled for morning and evening prayers. Around the edges of the room were small wooden lockers. Mine was Number 30 at the far end, just to the left of the double doors which led outside. There was a huge rubber covered staircase, running through the centre of the new wing, with a wire cage in the middle, rather like the sides of an old fashioned lift in a department store.

From the Common Room, you turned left towards the music rooms at the far end. There were probably ten cubicles. I cannot remember whether each one contained an upright piano or not. But I can recall the last cubicle on the left because that was where I went for my music lessons with Miss Amy Page. The lower ground floor consisted of a large drill room, shoe and cloakrooms and doors which led out to the lower playground, fields and gardens.

I thought the oak panelled dining room was lovely. It was

large, but not so overpowering for a small child only seven years old. There were two fireplaces at either end that always contained pretty flower arrangements. Four lower refectory tables and benches, were positioned close to the bay windows. A centre table at the narrowest part of the room, then widened to accommodate four more tables with benches for the taller girls.

How I longed to sit at the bigger tables! I only just made the centre ones, before world events intervened in 1939, ending any prospect of me advancing onto the top tables.

The Head Matron's office was to the left of the main entrance and the impressive wide oak staircase led up to the Headmistress's study and to dormitories Four, Five and Six, but of course that was not the way I went to bed.

Our lives were literally 'summoned by bells,' to borrow John Betjaman's words, from the rising bell, prayer, breakfast, linen room and assembly bells throughout the day. After breakfast, we all had a duty to perform. I was delighted to have the little bedroom to dust between my dormitory and Dormitory Five. It

Me standing under the rose arch, which I could see from the dormitory, wearing my brown cotton pinafore.

was always allocated to one of the two pupil teachers—girls from Rickmansworth who spent a year helping the staff before going on to teacher training college.

The bathrooms in the old wing were smaller and cosier than those in the new wing. These were so much larger with rows of wash basins with a small mirror above each one and a row of baths at the end. We all bathed according to a rota system. The dormitories were grouped together and the days alternated. Bath time was in the evening, but there was no time for soaking! Undressing, bathing and washing in front of everyone was no problem for me.

Then it was back to the dormitory, where we were expected to brush our hair and then get into bed with something to occupy us until it was time for lights out. And no talking! What a difficult rule that turned out to obey, particularly with Jackie on one side of the dormitory and Doreen on the other. Many an evening would go by with Miss Harrop, the Headmistress waiting for us all to be quiet and settled down. But if the member of staff on duty ever caught us talking and laughing, that was a very different matter. On went the lights and we were told, "Out of bed! Strip your bed—I still do every morning! Make your bed! Get back into bed!"

Then very often we would have to repeat the process all over again. By which time we had had enough and obediently went to sleep. Well, everyone else invariably slept, except for me. I was often awake between nine and ten o'clock.

How do I know? I used see the light from Miss Dunn's torch appear as she came along the corridor from Dormitory Three. Every night, the Head Matron went to each girl's bed to make sure that all was well, before she then turned in for the night. How long did it take her? I do not know of course, but it must have been quite some time. She had to go to 120 beds and right up to the top dormitory on the fourth floor of the new wing. Then she had to make her way back to her own bedroom at the far end of the old building. I know that we thought her a very strict disciplinarian. We did not appreciate that she was caring and looking after us, just like a mother looks in at her sleeping children before going to bed.

It was certainly not the Weybridge school clothes we liked, either the winter or summer ones! The first garment we always put on was our combinations. On top of this we wore a liberty bodice. It had rubber buttons on the sides and came to about hip length. It was on to these that we attached our brown woollen stockings with elastic loops and over all this we wore navy ETBs (elastic top and bottom knickers). A dark blue long sleeved serge dress was followed by a light brown double pinafore and the look was finished off with black lace up shoes. For special occasions, we had black button strap shoes. To go outdoors, we had dark navy velour coats and hats, with a simple plain navy gross grain ribbon with the circular school badge in the centre.

In the summer, the stockings became lisle knee length socks. The dress was a lighter blue cotton with short sleeves and we had panama hats. Amazingly I do not recall wearing a blazer at Weybridge, but I see in a letter to Mother that I had mentioned blazer badges to Miss Dunn.

On the rising bell, we got up, stripped back our beds, went to the bathroom and then back to the dormitory to brush our hair. According to the rules, hair had to be short and not touch the collars of our dresses. If it did, then it was put into bunches and if longer still, it was made into plaits. I was fortunate to have straight fine hair, so brushing and combing it was easy and fast. I was always ready by the time the next bell went. Not so Doreen. She had lovely thick long hair, which needed brushing and then plaiting. I recall her struggling on many occasions with one of the pupil teachers often helping her get ready. It was even worse for Doreen when we had hair washing, because it would take so very long for her hair to dry. Again this was organised on a dormitory

Mother's picture of me and my little group of friends—note the pinafores again! Jackie is next to me on the right.

rota system and the Matrons and pupil teachers were always on hand to help out. You may be wondering how we coped in an age before electric hairdryers? Well, fires were lit in the dormitories and we used to sit around on the floor behind the screens rubbing our heads with towels.

After breakfast and our duties, the linen bell rang. There was a linen room in each wing of the school. If we had any holes in our clothes or anything that needed repairing, we were expected to report to the Matrons who did the mending. I was fortunate in that I was not very heavy on my clothes, so I did not often wear holes in my stockings or socks, and rarely went to the linen room.

On Saturday, after the dinner bell rang, we assembled in the Common Room in our usual semi–circle. Miss Dunn would come in with a tray of sweets. This was our weekly sweet allocation of one penny worth. There was always a good selection to choose from. Round white peppermints, you got twenty four for a penny. Barley sugar sticks, you could suck these to a point and prick someone if you were feeling mischievous! And eighteen boiled sweets, these lasted at least until tea time on Sunday afternoon.

Then there were packets of other sweets, which because they were softer, were eaten very quickly indeed. But before we were allowed to go to the table and choose our selection, Miss Dunn would inspect each girl's clothes. Anyone with any holes was sent off to get them repaired.

On one particular Saturday, Miss Dunn found I had a hole in my stocking. I was obediently waiting outside the linen room door when Miss Dunn reappeared.

"What are you doing standing here Barbara Kelland? I hear that you can sew. Go and mend your own clothes."

Of course by the time I had finished repairing the offending hole and returned to Miss Dunn's office where I was inspected again—all the best sweets had gone and I could only choose the packets containing soft ones. It was a salutary lesson. I never missed the linen bell again. I made sure that I was always able to choose what I wanted. I was only eight years old.

My classroom was C1, at the far end of the old wing, next to the staircase that led up to Miss Dunn's room and Dormitory One. It was not very large and had a wooden floor, as did all the classrooms in the old wing.

Miss Harrop, the Headmistress, gave us lessons in elocution and verse speaking. We learnt deep breathing and to say correctly:

> How now brown cow, please tell me how you
> came to be a nice brown cow.

We had to make round 'O' sounds, speaking clearly and distinctly. I suppose having elocution lessons must seem very odd to most people today, and no doubt would be considered politically incorrect.

Next to this classroom was the quiet room. It had small wicker chairs, an aquarium (I thought this was lovely), around which many of our nature study lessons with Miss Moore were based. It had little book shelves and it was here that any girl could come and sit quietly to read. We also used to go there whenever we received a visit from our mothers. And so it was, one day in October 1936, that I sat there patiently waiting. This first encounter has always stayed with me, for as Mother appeared in the doorway, so the tears, always close to the surface, flowed freely down my face. I had not shed any in September, but by October I sobbed bitterly. Even Mother's mantra of KDC, "Kellands Don't Cry," did little to stem them.

We were allowed one visit a term from our mothers. Again I was fortunate that Mother lived in Surrey. She could make the journey for the few hours she was allowed to stay. In all my eleven years at the school, she never once failed to come.

When I moved up to C2, Miss Vaughan became my form teacher. She also taught us needlework. I can remember distinctly standing beside her while she instructed me in the basic method of hemming, the correct direction to hold the needle, thread and how to position my thumb.

Many, many years later, I was teaching my pupils in exactly the same way. At one of the Old Girls' reunions, I met Miss Vaughan and let her know that I was passing down to the

JUNIOR MASONIC SCHOOL,
WEYBRIDGE

Barbara Kelland

Report for Term ending Easter, 19 39

Form B1   Average Age 9 years 11 months

General Form Work Good on the whole.
Barbara has worked well, and
her spelling has much improved.

B. C. Earl   Form Mistress.

Conduct
Very Good

K. Harrop   Head Mistress.

School re-opens Monday, May 1st

One of my report cards for the Easter term, 1939.

younger generations her methods of sewing. Hemming was also used for sewing on tapes. Did we really need to learn how to sew these on? Yes we did, because we had to make a bag that taught us some basic needlework skills. It was tied around our waists, with tapes. We made a pattern on the hems in tacking, using a cotton thread and then we embroidered a picture on the front. We kept our sewing in this bag.

This second classroom in the old wing had a window, which overlooked part of the garden. My main memory is of the beautiful, very tall, deep blue delphiniums. I used to gaze at these flowers, probably when I should have been paying more attention to my lessons!

We had progressed to writing in ink. This involved having monitors who were required to see that the little ink wells in our desks were kept filled. This was a very responsible duty, because they had to take great care making sure not to spill any. The floors as I have mentioned, were plain wood and if any ink got split, it had to be cleaned up immediately with salt and lemon juice.

By 1938–39, I had reached the last of the classrooms in the old wing, Form B1. Miss Earl was the form teacher. My strongest memories of this time are of the wide range of handcrafts I was taught, as well as needlework and music.

In my letters home, I often referred to what I was making in handwork. There was no shortage of materials. I can still remember the back of the classroom door with large skeins of raffia hanging on it, of every colour imaginable. Not only did we learn weaving using basic Dryad Craft cards, but I learnt how to make containers with rope and raffia. I really enjoyed this. The stitches and patterns were all based on Indian and African themes. Many years later, when I was at teacher training college on my first long teaching practice, I decided to do my project with the class of nine year olds based on Longfellow's poem 'Hiawatha.' And yes, they made raffia and rope 'pots.'

I made Mother a flat fruit bowl, using blue and cream raffia. It was as large as a small dinner plate with shallow sides, probably just two rounds of rope. It took pride of place on her oak dresser to complement the blue and white china. Using the Dryad Craft weaving cards, we had a choice of making either a tea cosy or slippers. I chose a tea cosy. Mother kept it for many years, because it was a very good size. It was still in use, with a special cover to protect it, when she passed away at the age of eighty. I had used her favourite colour scheme of green and white with a touch of butter yellow. The lining was yellow (which showed all the tea stains!) and it was padded with wadding, not the polyester of today, but probably a flat kapok (like cotton wool).

We had of course, the correct weaving and raffia needles. In later years I would often reflect on this, as I was juggling with my requisition and trying to decide how to spend the few pounds my department had been allocated.

We used soft embroidery thread. It was easy to work with and there was a good range of colours. We learnt how to double warp the card and to fix warp threads to the small brass curtain ring in the centre of each side. The teacher worked out a pattern for us. I can vaguely recollect the basics of mine. Starting with green near the brass ring, I wove say ten lines of green, changed to yellow, wove three lines of yellow, two lines of white, three lines of yellow then back to a band of green.

In needlework too, there were more than ample supplies of fabrics and thread. Most of my memories are centred around articles made from linen. Unfortunately, none now exist, but the ideas proved a great resource for me in later years. I remember making a green tray cloth. The hems were held in place with a design in a cotton embroidery thread.

Here is a reference in one of my letters to making articles in handwork, dated April 4, 1937:

I am making something for you but I don't think I can bring it back this term, as I think I want it for Prize Day.

July 11, 1937.
I had three things up on Prize Day.

One of these was most probably a green linen drawn up bag. I do not recall any of the displays of work, but obviously they were in the classrooms.

We also had a lesson called drill, (PE today). I remember the teacher, Miss Crossland. She was not on the permanent staff and came into school to take the lessons, held in the Common Room or new wing drill room. My memory is very vague as to what we actually did. I know we were taught the basics of breast stroke. We lay over little stools, and went through the motions of co–ordinating our arms and legs correctly. I am sure we could all swim—I could by the time I went to the senior school at Rickmansworth, which had a lovely indoor pool.

I do remember Miss Crossland though. She seemed to us to be an old lady (as all teachers do to young children). She always dressed in a white blouse under a box pleated black tunic, tied at the waist with a girdle, black stockings and plimsoles. She was rather well built, with legs that always seemed too slender to support her body. She had a florid complexion and fuzzy black grey hair. I liked drill and used to try so hard, but the school prize always went to Jacqueline, who was better than me at all sports. The fact there was a drill room in each wing of the school, suggests that these rooms would also have been used for team games. I remember skipping competitions held in them.

In Miss Mary Moore's art lessons I learnt the basics of applying water colour washes and looking after brushes. My work was often on display and I received good marks. In July 14, 1938, I wrote:

> We are making a calendar in art and next term I
> might do a big picture for Miss Moore.

Well, I certainly did a big picture, with Jackie's help! It was of two people—hikers we called them—walking up the side of a mountain. Our work was obviously good enough for display. The teacher had it mounted on black paper with our names attached, probably under the figures. I had this painting folded up in a tea chest for years. By the time I rediscovered it in 2000, and sent it off to Jackie, the black paper had long since gone along with our names, so I never knew which one of us did which figure. I wonder if Jackie can remember?

We had special singing lessons and as far as I know, we were all taught to play the piano. I started with Miss Amy Page at an early age, probably when I was seven years old. But more about music later.

On Friday evenings after tea, we all went to our form rooms and here we wrote a copy letter to our mothers. Mother had kept a lot of these, which she received for the eleven years while I was at both the junior and senior Masonic schools. My letter would always arrive on a Tuesday morning. She wrote her reply, posted it on Wednesday, and I received it the following day, ready for me to start again afresh on Friday. This was a regular occurrence which was never once broken. What does a little seven year old write to her mother? I am sorry to say very little! In February 1938, I discovered that Miss Vaughan had instructed us to, 'write longer letters to our mothers.' It was only decades later that I found out Miss Vaughan was also a former pupil of the school.

In those early days, my letters were short and often appallingly spelt. The staff were very good in not correcting every mistake we made in our first copy letter. But then a little seven or eight year old does not always copy everything correctly either. Nevertheless, somehow Mother managed to understand what I was trying to express. Often a sentence says, 'Yes, I will try harder with my spelling.' Or, 'Yes, I will try not to make so many mistakes.' I can guess what Mother must have been writing back to me! Then there was always a request:

'My dear Mummy,

Please will you send me …' and the list followed. Sometimes it was stamp hinges for my album, or marbles, knitting wool and needles, sewing needles, scissors and coloured paper and glue, scraps of fabric, for I was always making things; knitting or sewing clothes for a teddy bear, making cards, taking something up to bed to sew.

It never once occurred to me that poor Mother would not have the time or spare money to buy my 'wants,' but as always the parcel arrived every week. The letters mention the names of lots of little friends. They often wrote to Mother and I am sure she replied. But one of the most recurring themes at Weybridge was the garden. Amongst my very first letters, I requested something for it:

> My Dear Mummy,
> Please Mummy will you geeper (sic) some
> morse pan (sic) and other things that you put in
> the cake. Please will you send me a nome (sic).

I was always writing about my little garden. Often moving things around, after asking for plants or bulbs or gnomes. This is my first letter to Mother:

> September 20, 1936.
> My Dear Mummy,
> Thank you so much for your letters.
> I am very happy here and hope to make a friend
> soon. We have gardens which we can share with
> our friends. Girls graw (sic) all kinds. One girls
> (sic) has a big sunflower which is much taller

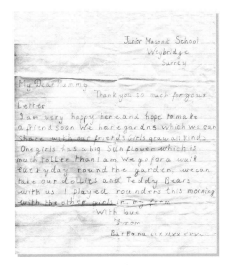

LEFT and ABOVE: An early letter home, complete with drawing of a 'nome.'

than I am. We go for a walk everyday round the garden. We can take our dollies and Teddy bears with us. I played rounders this morning with the other girls in my form.

With love from Barbara.

November 23, 1936.

My Dear Mummy,

Please Mummy will you send me some needle-work to do as I want to make a present for Xams (sic). I am making lots of Xams (sic) cards. We are making lanterns. I got the wool quite safely, and the gnomes, (now spelt correctly!) We made a house for them and put a stone in front of it and flowers round it and little sticks with moss on them and some violets.

I think our garden will look nice in the summer and have noticed two bulbs shoothing thsough (sic). I have started the scarf. I am going to write to Aunty Nell and Uncle John.

With love from Barbara.

November 29, 1936.

My Dear Mummy,

I have bought some toothpaste in shopping tonight. I have moved my garden and Vera has sent home for a gnome and I am sharing with Nora. Vera's garden is just next to our garden, it looks very nice. Vera's going to give me some bulbs and some crocuses. We have some primrose (sic) in each corner and a hause (sic) in the middle and some violets. We put some rose plants on the roof to make it look pretty.

Thank you very much indeed for the hanker-chiefs (sic). I like sewing the lace on very much. With tons of love from Barbara.

The gardens were a great source of enjoyment and interest as well as keeping us fully occupied. I do not remember how they were allocated, only that this was an activity I thoroughly enjoyed. 'The gardens' as they were known, were on a spare plot of ground at one end of the top playground. We were allowed to get water at the tap inside the kitchen gardens, which were just out of bounds. (We went in there when we were walking in our crocodile pairs around the grounds, often after tea. But only once the member of staff on duty, who was accompanying the walk along with the pupil teacher, had given her permission).

Somehow the poor plants survived. Perhaps they knew that the little girls who were digging them up, replanting and watering them, were happy and enjoying themselves at play. Then along with the next arithmetic exercise, the test results and the exams, a sentence would appear telling Mother of something different. As I have said, the daily, weekly, monthly routine was so ordered that anything, however insignificant to an outsider, was an important event and had to be told.

Letter December 13, 1936, written in pencil on lined paper:

> My Dear Mummy,
> We had a party and I was a robin and we had
> crackers. It is not very long before I will see you
> again. I had some new shoes today. I am looking
> forward to Thursday when I shall see you.
> With love from Barbara.

I was very interested to find this letter. I had always remembered the Christmas party, mainly because I was on the very top table where all the older girls usually sat. Why I was a robin and why we only ever had one party I do not know. But I was so pleased to read it because the Christmas party during that first term at Weybridge has remained one of my deepest held memories.

Later on Sunday, probably sometime during the afternoon, we went back to our classrooms and wrote a best letter to our mothers, copying out the one we had written earlier. It must have been during the Friday evening that we sent in our list for 'shopping' to our form teachers. We all returned to school with pocket money, which was handed in to cover our little requests. Poor staff! All these little lists of pencils, rubbers, glue etc, that they bought for us. Probably money for the postage stamps was taken out of our pocket money as well.

I see from the early years of 1936 and 1937, Mother had provided me with stamped address envelopes, which I am sure the form teacher would have kept. A recurring theme was the number of weeks and days until the end of term or until Mother was to come and visit me. Here is the final part of the letter written on April 14, 1937:

> ... it doesn't seem there is only a week to go,
> does it? and we will soon be having our home

clothes on our beds, won't we?
Love to Grandma and Grandpa.
With lots of love and kisses,
Barbara.

I had completely forgotten about the 'home clothes' on our beds, but I do remember where they were stored. They were taken away at the beginning of each term and placed in wardrobes in the attic areas of the old wing.

In reading through these early letters I learnt we had a 'rest time.' This was only a vague and hazy memory, but I mention it just casually on March 14, 1937, in a letter written in pencil on lined paper referring to Mother's birthday card:

> We can also write when we have a card to send
> to other people on their birthdays. I forgot to
> post yours on Tuesday, but I did send it on
> Wednesday morning at rest time.

Mother's birthday fell on a Wednesday in 1937, so she would not have received her card on time! And during that early period away at school, my mind still dwelt a lot on home life. In May 1937, I wrote '… and if I don't think about home, the days go by very quickly.'

The letter I produced on June 6, 1937 was very short! It explained my fear of reading aloud in front of the school.

> I did not go in for the poetry competition as I
> thought all the girls would be listening, but I am
> going in for it next time, for Miss Harrop told
> us, that the rest of us could not go and listen to
> the others. Is it fine in Worcester Park? It has
> been nice weather down here. We had our tea in
> the garden.

The part of the garden in question this time, would have been the grass area immediately outside the dining room. This was always known as the Mistresses's Lawn and we were not allowed to play on it, so having tea there was indeed something to write home about. In 1937, I think Easter must have been early. This letter is dated March 28.

> We had Easter eggs on Sunday morning for breakfast and hot cross buns on Saturday and Sunday afternoons and incense in church and a procession.

Every Sunday we would walk in our 'crocodile' pairs, down the hill to the parish church.

> March 27, 1938.
> It is only one week and six more days for the Waterloo girls. On Sunday it was Mothering Sunday. We went to church as well and there were lots and lots of people. There were flowers given out, there were daffodils, violets and primroses all in one bunch. The man who was the vicar of Appleton, came to talk to us. There were some flowers left over and some of the school had them.
> Love Barbara.

Another interesting occasion occurred in July 1938. The weather was very good, warm and sunny. The dinner bell sounded at the end of morning lessons and we assembled according to height in the Common Room. Our faces must have registered looks of amazement, concern and worry as we walked into the dining room, for the tables were not laid and there was not a sign of any food. No large trolley waiting to be unloaded—

nothing. I remember looking around and wondering what was going on? Where was our dinner? Where was our food? I must have always been hungry! We stood at our places as we usually did and the member of staff on duty said grace. We remained standing. No one had told us to sit down.

Suddenly the hatch between the dining room and the kitchen opened. In came the maids carrying trays on which were white paper bags filled with something. A tray was placed at the end of each table and the bags passed around. Imagine our surprise and delight when we opened them and looked inside. A packed lunch! I could hardly believe my eyes. Nothing like that had ever happened before.

We were told we could go down to the hay field. This was beside the lower playground and normally out of bounds. The grass had been cut and left to dry. We were allowed to have our lunch there and play. And so we passed a very happy day, eating and making hay houses of course! What was the occasion? It was Miss Dunn's birthday. This is the last sentence of my weekly letter home.

> On Miss Dunn's birthday we went in the hay
> field and had dinner out there too.
> All my love and kisses from,
> Barbara.

Reading these words, I am surprised I did not elaborate more, considering I can remember so well the impact that the empty dining room tables had made on me.

> November 14, 1937.
> My Dear Mummy,
> I hope you are well and that Mickey is behaving
> himself. We had a nice Armistice Day. We were
> silent for two minutes at 11am and we had

poppies too. Our form could only have penny ones but I did not mind.

The classroom looks very nice with the flowers in it, a little girl had visitors and put her flowers in with mine. I am on Test 3 in Arithmetic. I had a star for English 2 and a star for English 1. I am making something nice in handwork. Give my love to Grandma and Grandpa.
Love from Barbara.

I had not remembered that mothers brought flowers when they came to visit. My only memory was from 1937, when I would have been in Miss Vaughan's form, and fell over as I proudly carried in a beautiful glass vase, which broke of course. The flowers were probably the ones I had written home about. One letter in particular surprised me very much. I had to keep referring to the date to make sure it was correct.

September 25, 1938.
My Dear Mummy,
Yes, I have put my bulbs in the garden. I hope you are well and getting on all right. I am making something in handwork for you. Yes, I am going to try and work hard this term. For my duty I do a mistress's bedroom. I do hope you will get on in the evening classes. We have tried our gas masks on. I liked it. I have to have a small one. The eye piece is too low. When you write to Auntie Nancy again, give my love to the family.
Love to all,
Barbara.

In the next letter not dated but written on the same lined paper, I reply to Mother, 'Yes, let's trust we shall never have to wear the gas masks.' Strange now to think that we became quite accustomed to carrying our gas masks around. Not only had we been issued with them, but the public was told to put brown sticky tape in a criss cross pattern on all the windows of their homes.

At Weybridge, while we were all out at the cinema, the windows and glass panes in the doors were taped. Steadily preparations for war were being made as the political situation in Europe worsened. Hitler had declared the union of Germany and Austria and annexed the German speaking parts of the Sudetenland in 1938.

Mother was aware that the Bloomsbury Trade School was planning to leave London for Hertfordshire in the event of war being declared. She realised of course that she could not go with the rest of the school and so faced the prospect of unemployment yet again. Her cousins still lived in central London and were becoming anxious as well. They would be in great danger if they stayed on in the capital. There would have been considerable discussion I am sure, about the best way for them to leave. Since the trade school that employed Mother was run by the London County Council (LCC), she had a good idea of the plans that were being drawn up to evacuate London children to the countryside. And of course adults would be needed to accompany them.

Was this a possible exit strategy for Mother's cousins and aunt? They were all in rented accommodation, as they did not own a property like Mother and none of them had any children, so there were no ties. Maybe a way could be found to get them to safety.

It was not until I read a letter dated 16 October 1938, that I realised 'break' was referred to as 'recess' at Weybridge.

> Thank you for seeing about my watch and getting the glass put in, the gloves fit me lovely. I wear them every recess time and at practice after dinner.

I am sure that everyone who went to Weybridge, will recall recess. I took most of my lessons in the old wing and as a result, was always in the top playground. We had a lot of favourite games. I remember distinctly playing a ball game on the walls of the drill room. It went something like this:

1) Throw ball against wall and catch.
2) Bounce once to hit wall and catch.
3) Jump feet astride, throw ball from between legs.
4) Jump feet astride, back to wall, bounce ball between legs. Jump around to face wall and catch ball.
5) Face wall and throw ball around waist to wall using right hand and go around back, to left side.
6) Face wall same as 5, only ball in left hand and go around back, to right side.

When you dropped the ball it was someone else's turn. Then there was 'Two Ball.' This became more complicated and difficult, throwing two balls at the wall one after the other. Skipping was also a great favourite. I could skip very well and really enjoyed seeing how many 'bumps' I could do.

How can I describe 'bumps?' Skipping is simply two jumps as the rope turns. We then turned the rope faster and just did one jump, then turned the rope really fast twice and again only jumped once. This meant you had to jump much higher. And there was a chant to accompany the routine:

Missis M Missis I Missis S S I
B B Bump BB Bump BB Bump Bump Bump
Missis S Missis I Misses P P I
B B Bump BB Bump BB Bump Bump Bump.

Of course, if you tripped up then it was the next girl's turn. 'Keep the Pot Boiling' was another favourite. This was often played with the pupil teachers, probably when we were out in the playground for longer periods. It was usually a pupil teacher and maybe an older tall girl who turned the rope because it was very long. We lined up on one side of the person holding the rope, and as she turned it, we ran in under the loop and out at the other end, trying not to get caught as the rope came down. Then we went round the other side of the end girl, ready to go back again. This was continuous until one of us got caught and was therefore out. The last girl left was the winner.

Another game we played also involved a chant. We all ran into the centre of the rope, everyone chanting and skipping at the same time.

All in together girls
This fine weather girls
I spy a nanny goat
Hanging out her petticoat
OUT spells OUT!

And with that we had to run free of the rope. All generations of little girls have their own skipping games and variations on similar themes. This activity helped keep us occupied, healthy and accept the fact that we did not always win. Although we did not realise any of these things at the time. When we were not playing ball games, skipping or tending our gardens, 'Cat's Cradle' was another favourite. I was amused to see it on BBC World News as one of their computer generated images. Of course there were numerous other games children always make up. I loved to play marbles. I think it was the lovely colours and patterns that I liked, rather than the actual knocking out of another girl's marble. Then there were the Brownies. I really enjoyed being a Brownie and was an Elf. I was so delighted to find the following letter:

> June 4, 1939.
> My Dear Mummy,
> My Lupins in our garden have come out. I have about seven blue and one of the girls has a big Lupin plant and her flowers are pink. She had more than 25. I hope you are quite well. We have had some lovely blossom on the trees. We have had drill on the Mistresses's Lawn.
>
> In Brownies we had a game of Robin Hood and I was one of Robin Hood's men and we could go anywhere we liked in the garden but not across the drive and the others were Barons and they had treasure hidden all over them and we had to try and get it from them and if we touched them, they would have to count 50, while we were finding the treasure that was hidden on them and if we had not found it by the time they counted to 50, we would have to let them go.
>
> Please when you come to see me, don't forget to bring the camera with you, and remind Miss Dunn about me having to change into my

Brownie suit. I am doing a big picture with Jacqueline of hikers.
All my love,
Barbara.

My strongest memory as a Brownie, was being allowed 'out of bounds,' during the game of Robin Hood. Although what we actually played did not leave a lasting impression, it was more the fact I was running around in areas of the grounds where we were not normally allowed to go, that has stayed with me. And there were treats too. On November 8, 1936, I wrote:

> We had fireworks on Wednesday as we could not have them on Thursday as it was a Brownie meeting. We had lots of rockets and a nice bonfire.

On November 7, 1937, I only managed one sentence:

> We had fireworks on November 5th.

I liked fireworks and I can remember standing wrapped up in my coat on the lower playground, well away from the gardeners, who were setting them off. Strangely enough there is no letter from November 1938. I was surprised by this, because that particular November, was the one none of us who were at the school have ever forgotten.

How do I know? Because in 1990 at the Old Girls' Day reunion, Mary, Margaret, Pat and myself were having tea in the Dining Hall at Rickmansworth. The talk turned to Weybridge and inevitably to November '38. We all remembered it very well indeed and there was no need to ask the reason why. One of the girls Nellie, had lost her velour hat. I do not remember how Matron discovered that the hat had gone missing, but she knew

LEFT: me in my Brownie uniform. ABOVE: Brown Owl right, and Tawny Owl left, (Miss Wright and Miss Vaughan). BELOW: my Brownie test card.

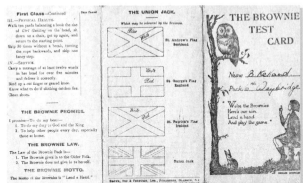

all right. We were told to search our dormitories and if we did not find Nellie's hat, then there would be no fireworks the following day. We looked everywhere and no one found the missing object. So naturally the punishment was carried out.

On Bonfire Night we all reported to our classrooms, probably for silent reading. I remember sitting listening to the fireworks going off all around us in Weybridge and feeling very left out. But that was not the end of the matter, for the next day, the hat miraculously materialised. Nellie had hidden it, I think somewhere in the bathroom near her dormitory. When I saw what the hat looked like, even at my young age, I realised why the poor girl did not want to wear it. I do not think I would have wanted to either. Whereas my hat and most of the others were traditional (like a Panama) Nellie's was a pork pie shape. But amazingly, that punishment has stayed lodged in all our memories, even after the passage of five decades! Of course we did not know in November 1938, that by the following year, we would be experiencing fireworks of quite a different kind.

Then there was the cinema trip in 1938 to see the first release of Disney's production of 'Snow White and The Seven Dwarfs.' The only memory I have is walking along in 'crocodile' pairs. But on May 29, 1938, I wrote to Mother:

> Yes, 'Snow White and the Seven Dwarfs' are still
> going on, I know.

Visiting the cinema would have been an exciting afternoon out for us. And that same year, brought another memorable occasion. It was during the summer term when we were told to go to the Common Room and sit in our usual sizes in a semi–circle. On the table in front of us, was a tray containing a large number of small rectangular shapes. Always thinking of my stomach, I thought they must be edible, because to my eyes they looked just like blocks of ice cream that we used to put between two wafers. The

Headmistress of Rickmansworth, Miss Bertha Dean was sitting in a chair. This lady had a fearsome reputation, probably handed down from sisters at the senior school, to younger ones at Weybridge. I know that I viewed her with a certain amount of apprehension. What was she doing at Weybridge? Why had she come to speak to us?

I do not recall what she talked about. I only remember going up to the table and receiving one of those small white boxes. For that is what they turned out to be—and inside? Well, there was a silver brooch with the lovely school badge in the centre. This was to commemorate the Masonic School's 150th anniversary. I wore my brooch for many years after I left school, until the clasp broke, which I am pleased to say has since been mended. This was a generous act on the part of the Masons and I have always appreciated it.

In the same letter, I am writing about Miss Dunn's birthday and dinner in the hay field. I just managed one sentence:

> No, I did not win a prize but I won the potato race. I might run on Thursday. You said the same as Miss Dean.

I imagine that Mother was telling me what an honour it was to have received the brooch and how I should take care of it, obviously something similar to Miss Dean when she had spoken to us.

I remember that everything at Weybridge was of the best quality. The school literally shone. The floors were highly polished. So were the oak dining tables. Everywhere was spotlessly clean, just as we were supposed to be or nearly! Yet I never saw any of the people who were cleaning the school or cooking in the kitchen. We only knew Ivy, the head maid. She wore a black dress and starched white apron and cap. Ivy was a large lady and carried herself like a ship in full sail, as she wheeled the trolley through our dining room to where the staff ate their meals.

There were always potted plants on the tables and flowers in the big fireplaces. A great deal of attention was paid to detail and as far as we were concerned as little girls, everything in our lives ran smoothly. If we had a cold we would be looked after. Sometimes we were sent to the Sanatorium, other times we would be put to bed in the dormitory.

At the beginning of my second term at Weybridge, Miss Dunn added at the end of my weekly letter to Mother the following, just to let her know everything was all right:

> Barbara has a slight cold. So I am keeping her in bed for a day or two. She is otherwise well and quite happy. I will let you know when she returns to school.
> D O Dunn

As I mentioned earlier, I had a deformed left rib and by May 1938, I had to do exercises for it. On May 15, there is just one sentence in my letter referring to this: 'Yes, I do like exercises and they are not hard.' What were these exercises? I had to report to the Sanatorium every morning or maybe two or three times a week and hung from wall bars in one of the rooms. I am sure there were other exercises to do, but it is the hanging on the bars I remember best.

As the term became shorter and going home day got nearer, I dreaded the outbreak of an infectious disease that would prevent me from leaving the school. I had not realised that our mothers would have been informed of any infection. Similarly, it became quite normal at the end of the holidays to make the long walk to our doctor's surgery in Worcester Park.

This became a routine for the eleven years I was at both the

Weybridge and Rickmansworth schools. Our health was always being checked and we had to return at the beginning of term with a medical certificate. I became quite accustomed to all the medicals and trips to the dentist. Girls went to the Sanatorium for

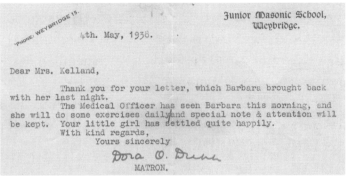

By kind permission of the Royal Masonic School for Girls

their doses of cod liver oil and malt. I often wondered why I was not given a spoonful, but I am sure the girls who had to take this medicine did not like it at all. The malt helped, but I do not think it disguised the cod liver oil taste very successfully!

During these first three years at Weybridge I had started to learn the piano. Miss Amy Page was my tutor. The music room was divided into little cubicles, each one containing an upright piano. We had a special time during the day when we were expected to practice. On the left hand side, at the far end was Miss Page's cubicle. I do remember sitting with her there, having lessons. We also had a percussion band and I became the conductor in the summer term of 1937.

> I think we are going to have school socks for Prize Day. I must keep my strap shoes nice at the back because I have my back to the audience.

That was all the explanation Mother received about the fact I was the conductor, a position I occupied for a long time. In

October 1937, I told her:

> I am trying hard at my music. I have got another
> book and the piece in it is called 'Buy my
> Balloons,' it is a very pretty piece.

And by December 12, I am writing to tell Mother that I played
in a concert. I had to perform a little minuet, 'Swing in the
Branches' and 'Buy my Balloons.'

> There was a man called Mr Ching. He could
> play lovely, I only wish I could play like it. He
> went so fast too, you could hardly see which
> notes he was playing. We have started exams.
> We have had English and writing. (Exams were
> held at the end of each term, for we were always
> being tested in every subject).

I remember Mr Ching performing for the whole school. It
seems strange that if this was the only occasion, I did not mention
the fact there had been a power failure and he played the piano
by candle light. It was the candles I can recall so vividly and later,
Mr Ching was to have an important impact on my career. In
October 1938, at the end of a very short letter, I wrote:

> I might go to Murdochs, which is in London. If
> I go, I will play 'Sea Horses' and 'A Toy The
> Albatross.'

Well, I did go. I remember walking along Oxford Street and
there were marvellous grand pianos in the shop windows. The
next impression has stayed with me very vividly. The concert was
to take place on the first floor and as we were going along the
corridor we passed a room. The door was wide open, the room in

'PHONE: WEYBRIDGE. 15.

24.7.38.

Junior Masonic School,
Weybridge.

Dear Mrs. Kelland,

This last case of chicken - pox was on July 23rd
At present Barbara is quite well and if she is unable to
travel on Wednesday a telegram will be sent. No girl who
is known to be ailing will be sent home; great care is taken
about this.

With kind regards

Yours sincerely

Dora O. Dunn Matron

Children who are being fetched from School should be called
for after 2.30 P.M. on Wednesday, 26th July.

Children who are being met at Waterloo will be taken to that
station on Wednesday, 26th July, and must be met in the Booking
Hall, NOT at the ticket-barrier at 3.20 P.M.

The Royal Masonic Institution for Girls,

JUNIOR SCHOOL, WEYBRIDGE.

25 2 19 38

DEAR Mrs. Kelland

The Easter Holidays

will begin on Friday 8 April

and the School will re-assemble on Tuesday
3rd May

Will you kindly acknowledge this note, and let me know
if you wish me to make any travelling arrangements for your
daughter.

Yours truly,

DORA O. DUNN,
Matron.

All Children must return on the day the holidays
terminate, except in case of illness, when a Medical Certificate NB.
NB must be sent (on that day) instead, or the Child will not be
re-admitted without the sanction of the House Committee.

C.H.—7670-36.

ABOVE, MIDDLE and LEFT: our health was always being checked, and the school made sure I returned at the beginning of a new term with a medical certificate.

total darkness except for a small square of light, which appeared suspended in mid air. We carried on, not stopping. But the memory of the light has remained with me. It was the screen of an early television set.

I am surprised I did not mention the fact to Mother, that apart from playing my three pieces, I was also the bass part in a trio, with Margaret Davies and Olwen Evans, both older than myself. Until I found the programme, I had not realised I was one of the youngest pupils, and the three of us were prize winners.

By the time I had reached Form B1, with Miss Earl as my teacher, I was still the conductor of the band and solo triangle. In December 1938, I remember having this very large triangle but not playing it! Yes, conducting the band came very naturally to me and I did not seem to mind standing alone in front of everyone.

Sometime in 1939, I was given a dulcimer. The piece I had to play, using two harmonies was 'Poor Old Joe.' In order to practice this new instrument I was allowed into the pupil teacher's room in the old wing. This was just by the stairs that led up to the dormitories and Miss Dunn's room. Poor Miss Dunn! After suffering hours of hearing the same tune being repeated over and over again, with all the mistakes, she came in and asked if I would not mind practising elsewhere! On Prize Day I opened the concert playing 'Poor Old Joe.' I know that I had to sit in front of the percussion band, on the right. I was higher than everyone else and facing the guests, who were in the rest of the Common Room. Everything must have been all right and perhaps I was not too nervous! It was much easier conducting the band, which I did after I had finished playing the dulcimer.

I am surprised that I have made no mention of this, but I think perhaps Mother was there that year. Jackie received the Drill Prize and when I found the programme I sent it to her. I knew that she would have liked to keep it. It is strange we did not play our trio. This threesome of little girls 'in blue,' had captured people's imaginations. For in the summer of 1939, I am writing to Mother:

> Miss Earl says that I might be playing the piano
> on Children's Hour, but it would probably not
> be possible because Margaret and Olwen are
> going up to Rickmansworth.

I was delighted to find this next letter, because the episode which follows was to have a prolonged effect on me, though naturally I did not realise it would at the time.

The prize winners from monthly Murdochs concerts, went on to play at the Wigmore Hall. In July 1939, my turn had come. This was to be quite an occasion. I am sure Mother gathered as many family members as possible. As they all lived in London, this would have been easy, but I have no recollection of who was there or even if I saw Mother at the concert. The beautiful piano was to the left of the stage. Since I was playing the bass part, I was furthest away from the audience. The three of us sat down. We knew what we had to do because we had practised many, many times. Olwen in the centre would count us in, then we would start playing. What followed has remained permanently embedded in my memory. Olwen said, "One, two, three, four," then, "No, no … let's start again."y

Margaret for some reason, she did not hear Olwen's last comment and carried on playing. Olwen did not repeat herself and started next and then I joined in, last of all.

The noise we produced was truly dreadful!

I did not have the confidence or experience not to start, which would have been much better. Mother said that my face became longer and longer. Why, oh why were we ever allowed to go on? Why did someone not just step out from the wings, tell us to stop and gently count us in again? Instead, we had to suffer utter embarrassment and a great humiliation. It would not happen today I am sure. An adult would have got up onto the stage and

MURDOCHS MONTHLY CONCERTS for CHILDREN

First of the Seventh Series
SATURDAY 12th Nov. 1938

Commencing at 3 p.m.

ADJUDICATOR OF PRIZES

MR. JAMES CHING, M.A., F.R.C.O., MUS. BAC. (Oxon)

MURDOCHS MUSIC ROOM
461/463 OXFORD Street · London · W1

LEFT and BELOW: the programmes for Murdochs who were piano sellers on Oxford Street. They held monthly piano competitions for children. The winners ended up at the Wigmore Hall, later in the year.

EXTRACT FROM
A LETTER RECEIVED FROM
SIR HENRY J. WOOD

August, 1935.

In my opinion, the Murdoch Monthly Piano Concerts for Children are excellent.

They afford an opportunity to these young musicians of showing what they can do in public. They create a different atmosphere from the Competitive Festival and bring out a notable quality in their playing, only to be obtained by playing before their teachers, their fellow students and the public.

Long may they continue to prosper.

I shall always remember the enjoyable and instructive afternoon of July 6th, 1935, when I heard such a high standard maintained from twenty-seven of these sincere and keen little performers.

HENRY J. WOOD,
Queen's Hall, London, W. 1

These Concerts are under the Patronage of
Sir JOHN B. McEWEN   Sir LANDON RONALD
Sir GRANVILLE BANTOCK   Mr. E. STANLEY ROPER
Mr. TOBIAS MATTHAY   and   Sir HENRY J. WOOD

1 (a) THE SWING .. .. *Adam Carse*
   (b) DARBY AND JOAN (c) THE POSTMAN .. .. *Dunhill*
   Michael Posver (aged 6)
   (Miss G. M. Ogilvie, L.R.A.M., Kingsdown Avenue, S. Croydon.)

2 (a) ETUDE (b) FROLIC from "The Path of Progress" .. ..
   Marion Smith (aged 7)
   (Miss M. L. Duke, L.R.A.M., M.R.S.T., Albert Road, Buckhurst Hill.)

3 (a) UNDER THE BOUGH .. .. *D. Gray*
   (b) MOUNTAIN STREAMS .. .. *Gaynor Blake*
   (c) VALSE .. .. *Stuart Duncan*
   Margherita Bordi (aged 7)
   (Miss A. Maxwell, Cavendish Road, Brondesbury.)

4 (a) A TOY from "Early Elizabethans" .. .. *Anon*
   (b) THE ALBATROSS (c) SEA HORSES .. .. *Joan Last*
   Barbara Kelland (aged 9)
   (Miss A. Page, Masonic School, Weybridge.)

5 (a) MUSETTE .. .. *Bach*
   (b) ECOSSAISE .. .. *Beethoven*
   (c) RUSTLING LEAVES .. .. *Renée Miles*
   Elizabeth Triling (aged 9)
   (Miss V. Adamoff, L.R.A.M., The Avenue, Bedford Park.)

6 (a) RONDO from Sonatina, Op. 34 .. .. *A. Andre*
   (b) BOURÉE from Six Elementary Sketches .. .. *C. V. Stanford*
   Millicent Higton (aged 10)
   (Miss O. A. Ormerod, Masonic School, Weybridge.)

7 (a) MINUETTO, Op. 42, No. 3 .. .. *Hummel*
   (b) MUSETTE IN D .. .. *J. S. Bach*
   Sybil Bastien (aged 10)
   (Miss A. F. D'Amato, Bentinck Road, Yiewsley.)

8 (a) LITTLE DONKEYS WITH RED SADDLES .. .. *Adair*
   (b) AN OLD ROUND (Trio with Barbara Kelland and Olwen Evans) .. *Sampson*
   Margaret Davies (aged 10)
   (Miss A. Page, Masonic School, Weybridge.)

9 (a) LAVENDERS BLUE (b) DERRY DOWN DERRY (c) NEDDY TO THE FAIR
   (d) WEE WILLIE WINKIE .. .. *C. Lloyd*
   Thelma Hoare (aged 10)
   (Miss M. Holland, L.R.A.M., A.R.C.M., King's Road, Wimbledon.)

10 (a) MARCH IN D .. .. *Bach*
   (b) MUSETTE .. .. *Bach*
   (c) A SAILOR'S DANCE .. .. *T. F. Dunhill*
   Thomas Stone (aged 10)
   (Mrs. E. Orihashi, Hatfield Road, St. Albans, Herts.)

11 (a) TWO MINUETS IN G .. .. *Bach*
   Olwen Evans (aged 10)
   (Miss A. Page, Masonic School, Weybridge.)

INTERVAL.
During which a short Talk will be given on Bach's Favourite Keyboard Instruments

put the little girls out of their misery. What went on afterwards? I have no idea. All my other memories have been erased. Just those few awful moments remain, nothing else.

I obviously enjoyed my time at Weybridge. I had many little friends and really liked my garden and the hours I spent there. Since I had inherited the ability to use my hands, I was happy with all the craft subjects. I realised how fortunate I was to have the opportunity to learn all these things. And of course music, there was always music throughout my school life.

The staff provided and cared for us as far as our physical wants, health and education were concerned, but there was no pastoral care that I can recall. There was no one we could turn to and discuss any personal problems and worries, offering guidance or simply a sympathetic ear. We just had to get on with life as best we could. In the 1930s no one thought it was necessary, after all we were educated by people who themselves had been educated by the Victorians.

This may sound rather critical, but it is not meant to be. The ladies on the teaching staff were kind, considerate and dedicated to us. Some girls like myself, would attend both the junior and senior schools. I spent a total of eleven years between the two. But the staff gave their adult lives in the service of the school. Many of them, such as Miss Mildred Harrop and Miss Isobel Vaughan, both headmistresses at Weybridge, had been old girls themselves and would have understood the little girls in their care.

I recall one incident very clearly that Mother recounted to me, which demonstrated how we were treated even-handedly. Not long after arriving at Weybridge I caught a cold. Maisie, my cousin, sent me some tissues, which were immediately taken away by Matron. Other little girls did not have tissues, so I could not have any either. This would have been considered favouritism or excessive pampering. Mother on the other hand had always carried out to the letter, the instructions she received

ABOVE RIGHT: letter
from Miss Dunn, forward-
ing tickets to Mother.
ABOVE and RIGHT: the
Programme from the
Concert. I am playing with
Margaret and Olwen, 'The
Chase' and 'Polish Dance.'

from Great Queen Street in London, (the headquarters of the institution), when they stated:

> If a girl has any special personal possessions or some favourite play thing, these may be brought if desired. She may also bring, if she has them, a dressing gown, bedroom slippers, Bible and a Prayer Book and some note paper and stamps.

At Bloomsbury, Mother had a woollen dressing gown made for me in Masonic blue. She also bought a leather bound Bible, and clutching all this and a Teddy bear, I had arrived at Weybridge—exactly as the rules allowed for.

Maybe it was just my way of dealing with things. Some children find it easy to chat and confide in an adult. I obviously did not and was always wary of people. Soon, my little life at Weybridge was about to come to an end and a whole new set of challenges would open up before me.

WORCESTER PARK
1936–39

Worcester Park, 1936

The year 1936 was a memorable one for Mother. Not only had she visited her childhood friend in Ireland, but I was received into the Masonic School at Weybridge. She must have prepared me over a long period for the day when I was to leave home. I do not know how she did this. Perhaps my stay in hospital in 1934 when I had my tonsils out and Mother's holiday in Switzerland the following year, had got me used to being away from her. This is a brief account from Mother's diary, September 15, 1936:

> Shall I ever forget it? You were happy as a bird and I was taking you to school, you would be sleeping away from me and your home. You were most anxious to get there and you were not a bit downcast. You were carrying out what we both said we would do, and you were helping me to earn more money by settling down so well to your new life. Also you were going to have an education, that I could never hope to have been able to give you. And another thing, if I should be called away from you, you would still be safe 'till your school days were

over and I did so want you to have a happy childhood. Life to me though has now become lonely again and I only live for my letters from you, visiting day and your holidays.

I visited you some time later and oh what a surprise I got! Why, this could not be the slim little girl I said goodbye to, this couldn't be Barbara—but it was. You had grown fat, would you believe it? And you looked the picture of good health and happiness. I had not expected to see such a change. You showed me all over your beautiful school.

I thought it was interesting that I had put on weight. I was obviously being well fed at Weybridge. My weight gain was not due to a sedentary life style though—far from it. We were always encouraged to be out in the fresh air, running, skipping and playing games. We went regularly for walks in the grounds and also around Weybridge. It was probably the vast contrast between my home and school diets that accounted for the difference.

Mother appreciated the fact that since I was away from home and so well looked after, I was no longer a drain on the family purse. My wants were really minimal. I had a tartan kilt that I wore with the scarlet jumper from Kingsley High School. I wore the kilt for years during the winter holidays. Instead of it resting at my waist and therefore reaching probably my ankles, Mother had made a bodice so it started really under my armpits—and as I grew so the little bodice was lengthened.

During this time and the following year, Mother continued to teach at Bloomsbury Trade School and to take corset repair work from Waring & Gillow's. As I was away from home, she had more time to do all the preparatory work.

In 1933, just after moving from London she wrote in her diary:

> I have been going backwards and forwards to
> the Trade School, twice per week, since you
> were born. There was no money unless I earnt
> it. I only had the widow's pension of ten
> shillings and five shillings for you per week.
> There is such a lot of home preparation to do for
> the class, that I always seem to be working.

Mother never stopped trying to improve her lot in life. In 1938, she taught two evening classes on lingerie with the London County Council (LCC), and at the same time started a needlework evening class at Battersea Polytechnic.

Within the group, she was the only person from the world of trade. The rest of the class had already qualified as teachers and she was hoping to become a sewing teacher herself. This course would have provided her with a way into the profession, offering the prospects of a secure job and pension. She passed the first year with flying colours, easily coming top of the group and was looking forward to completing the course in the theory of education the following year.

But it was not to be.

In September 1939, after Hitler refused to withdraw from Poland, Britain declared war on Germany and all such training courses stopped. Mother's hopes of improving the quality of her life, were frustrated once again.

In August 1939, we had gone back to Ireland for another special holiday, this time with Mother's childhood friend Alice (Cissy) Godden. (We used to spend our summer holidays in England with Cissy's mother in Southsea).

Now the three of us left for Northern Ireland in Cissy's Austin Seven. It was great fun, with a lot of laughter as Cissy had a great sense of humour and a very infectious laugh. It would be her first return to Blacksod, where she and Mother had played together as little girls. We all enjoyed what was to be our last holiday for a very long time.

It was not many weeks after our return that I found myself sitting in my Grandfather's chair, waiting to hear an announcement from the Prime Minister, Neville Chamberlain.

The date was September 3, 1939.

Grandmother and Mother were also there, and we all sat beside the wireless waiting for Big Ben to strike eleven o'clock. No one knew what to expect. The French doors and windows had already been taped. Blackout curtains were made and ready for the windows. The upright piano had been moved away from the wall and placed at an acute angle to the window.

We listened to Chamberlain's speech in silence and I do not recall the adults' reaction to his statement that, "… this country is now at war with Germany," because the air raid sirens sounded immediately. They made a very frightening noise and Mother immediately put me into the apex between the piano and the wall. I sat on a chair with my favourite toys. Next came Grandmother and last of all Mother.

Almost immediately we heard aircraft directly overhead.

This was very unnerving as no one knew whether these were enemy planes or not. I remember sitting there, looking up at the ceiling and wondering what was going to happen. But all was well, as we later learned that these were RAF planes and there were no more alerts that day.

After the declaration of war, school children started to be evacuated from London. As expected, the Bloomsbury Trade School was relocated to Welwyn Garden City in Hertfordshire. Mother with her responsibility for Grandmother, her little house and me, was unable to move and found herself in the uncomfortable position at the age of forty, out of work.

Because so many children were leaving the capital, the LCC needed extra adults who were prepared to accompany them during the journey. Mother used her contacts on the council to successfully find places for her three cousins.

Nellie, the eldest was sent to Hitchen, Hertfordshire. Maisie was billeted with the village policeman and Doris went to live in rooms above a butcher's shop in Ashwell. Whenever I visited, I was given the job of reconstituting the powdered egg and generally helping Doris, who was a very keen and able cook.

It was also whilst I was at my cousins that I caught the 'bug' for preserving fruit. The war was in its early months and I had been instructed to look after my Grandmother who was visiting her sister in Hitchen. We had gone on the 'Green Line' coaches, probably from Victoria station. The journey seemed to last all day, but eventually we arrived.

While Maisie and I were walking around the village we came across a group of cherry plum trees. I was absolutely delighted that we could just pick the plums up from the ground and take them back to the billet, where the policeman's wife showed me how to bottle them. This started me off on something I was to continue with all my adult life.

When I returned to Surrey, I remember being so excited about bottling fruit. Although 'Kilner' brand jars would no doubt have been available, they were too expensive. Instead we used one pound jam jars. We could buy very reasonably priced metal tops, 'Porosan' was the brand name, that fitted over the jar (with a rubber ring round the rim), a strip of metal kept this in place and folded back at each side. This had to be pulled onto the top of the jar and centred, to ensure that the metal disc with the rubber seal was held firmly in place. In order to preserve the fruit, the bottles were placed in a very large saucepan half filled with water, which was then boiled. Or an alternative way, was to cook the fruit, apples for example, warm the sterilised bottles in the oven, fill the jars and carefully seal them with their metal tops.

Mother of course, enjoyed doing this as well. And by 1944, I was writing to her from school, saying how glad I was that she was bottling more fruit and I expected to see a shelf full of jars by the time I came home.

With the evacuation of the Bloomsbury Trade School to Hertfordshire, Mother was faced with the stark reality of being without a source of income again. The repair jobs from Waring & Gillow's stopped, as did any kind of private client work.

It is hard to imagine how she felt. Since Father's death she had struggled to improve her financial position and tried to obtain a professional qualification. Now it looked like all her efforts would count for nothing.

I had to return to school and Mother needed to find work. She had received notification from the Headmistress, informing her that she did not have to send me back to school if she felt worried, but Weybridge was as safe as anywhere else in the country—so that was at least a positive and one less thing for her to worry about. Unemployment benefit at the time was four shillings and sixpence a week. Fortunately Mother had her small savings to help her through the tough weeks and months ahead. How anyone managed without money to fall back on, I do not know.

But despite the Headmistress's assurances, the Masons took the decision to close the junior school for the duration of the war. I was very disappointed not to be returning to Weybridge. Looking back now, I feel sure that not only would my school work have improved greatly, but my development as a young person would also have been advanced had I stayed on. I was so looking forward to being in one of the top two forms. But now the prospect of the awesome senior school at Rickmansworth awaited me—a full year before I was really ready.

RICKMANSWORTH
1939–40

Rickmansworth, 1939

It was another September day, only this time the year was 1939 when Mother and I walked up the tree lined avenue from Rickmansworth railway station towards the school. The warming sun, filtered through the leaves. There was a vastness about the fields that spread out to my right. I continued with a growing sense of trepidation.

We had got about a third of the way along the avenue, when I saw them. Only faintly at first, then all of a sudden much more clearly. They were straight ahead of me, row after row of them, like pale blue eyes that could not stop staring.

A feeling of dread came over me. I bowed my head and moved closer to Mother's side, clutching her hand even more tightly. At last we stood before the great wrought iron gates.

We had arrived at the Royal Masonic Institution for Girls at Rickmansworth Park, Hertfordshire.

I can only start to imagine as an adult, what preparations and upheaval the staff of both schools had to face that September. The Weybridge girls had all been allocated to one of the eight identical houses. Jackie and Doreen from Dormitory Four at Weybridge were still with me in Zetland House, where we were to remain until we left school.

It was usual to begin classes in the middle of the week, but for the first few days, we were all left very much to our own devices. We still wore home clothes and spent the time making up games. My clearest memory is of trying to walk around the columns of the cloisters without touching the ground, going from Ruspini to Cumberland House.

The Weybridge girls all slept in number Four Dormitory with the fourth Prefect and Sub–Prefect. We did not realise it at the time, but these were the beds sent up from the junior school. This would have meant a reorganisation of the senior girls sleeping arrangements. There were fifty senior girls to each House and now they had to accommodate another fifteen little ones.

I found it very frightening being surrounded by hundreds of adults. All the seniors seemed so large and there were so many of them. This was very different from the much smaller school I had been used to of 120 girls at Weybridge. The 'blue eyes' that had filled me with so much anxiety, turned out to be the painted windows of the bathrooms, which had been blacked out in all the washing areas.

In every House there were four dormitories, each with its own bathroom. This consisted of a row of washbasins, two small rooms each with a bath and separate toilet. Later the baths had a painted blue line between the taps and the plug and because of wartime restrictions on the use of coal for heating, we could only fill the bath as high as this line.

The Freemasons as always had made good preparations in the event of war being declared. The organising skills and attention to detail required to cover every known eventuality well before September 3, were evident in the smooth (for the pupils at least) transition period during the first week back at school. On September 17, I wrote to Mother:

> As you know I am at Zetland House. It is very nice. I sleep in Dormitory Four. All the houses

are built in the same style. We wore home clothes until Saturday night. We have been down the trenches three times.

I have seen the swimming bath and the gym room. The dining room is very big. We have our own tables from Weybridge here. All the Weybridge girls have their prayers in the gym room with Miss Harrop. We have had an air raid practice from the Chapel. It is a lovely place.

We have not started lessons, but we will start on Monday. I have got locker Number 38.

Please will you send me my stamp album and bathing costume and cap. (I was obviously anticipating swimming lessons).
Love, Barbara.

The trenches had already been built before we arrived—though I should really call them shelters, but we referred to them as trenches. They were located alongside the road that led up from the Dell and passed behind Zetland and Ruspini Houses. There was a large mound at each end and in between were several entrances. Each trench was separate from the others. (The diagram of trench C that I drew in my letter of October 22, 1939, is reproduced on the next page). We had a lot of air raid drills. The Zetland House fire alarm would ring when the drill was from the House, this ensured of course that we would know and be familiar with what we had to do, where we had to go and how we were expected to cope.

The dining room at Rickmansworth was most impressive. It was a vast hall with a huge ceiling, beautiful refectory tables each

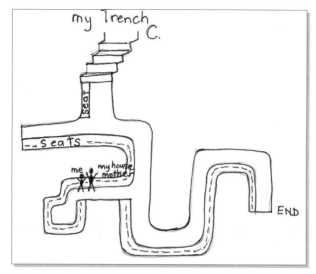

LEFT: this was the diagram of trench C that I drew in one of my letters. The trenches were underground and pitch black inside. Later I was to receive the Drawing and Painting prize!

with a potted plant in the centre and of course, always a grand piano. We sang grace at the beginning and end of each meal. I learnt later that not only was there a member of staff on duty in the hall but there was also someone outside in the quadrangle listening for the air raid siren.

Letter extract:

> We had an air raid drill on Tuesday afternoon and when the sirens went on Sunday, Miss Potter rang the bell in the middle of dinner. We had to get our gas masks out and go down to the trench. When we got outside we could hear the sirens.

This kind of interruption to meal times was not unusual. Once I was leaving the Dining Hall carrying a plate of food and finished it, sitting in the trench. The bread baskets followed and somehow the change of setting stimulated a fresh appetite. These times must have been worrying for the staff. They had the responsibility of ferrying over five hundred girls from a noisy hall to the trenches, in an orderly, sensible and quiet manner. And the air raid drills continued even after we had gone to bed.

> Letter in June:
> We had an air raid practice on Friday night at
> eleven o'clock when we were all asleep.

Now there was a definite procedure we had to adopt if the alarm went off after we had gone to bed. We had to: get out of bed, put on shoes, top coat, pixie hood, gas mask, (in its cardboard box) strip one blanket from our bed, put it around our shoulders, and then line up in numerical order in front of the swing doors in the dormitory and wait until told to file out of the side door nearest to the Senior Prefect's study room, across the area between the houses, over the road and into entrance C of the trench.

Because it was immediately behind Zetland House, we did not have far to go, unlike the girls from the houses on the opposite side of 'The Garth,' Athol and Cumberland. As we were juniors from Weybridge, we all had a senior girl, a 'House Mother,' to look after and sit beside us.

The trenches were very well prepared. There was a line of benches going all the way around the right hand side, two strips of wood served as a back rest from the wall, and duckboards were placed on the ground. There was a form of electric light and I am sure the walls and roof must have been supported with wooden boards. Trench C had several cul–de–sacs and we would not have been expected to find our way to these furthest ends in complete darkness.

There was one exception that remains very vividly in my mind. The fire alarm had sounded to signify an air raid warning. I was fast asleep and had not heard it. I awoke suddenly to find everyone getting out of bed. In my befuddled state, instead of getting into my air raid clothes, I hastily put on my blue dressing gown and slippers, stripped my bed (normal procedure on rising in the morning) managed to pull off a blanket and went to take my place in the queue by the door.

Nobody in Zetland remarked on my dressing gown until we were heading out of the House and across to the trench, and the girls from Ruspini House and others, were all gesticulating at me and making fun of my dressing gown. Whatever age we are, we never forget being ridiculed and how at that moment, I wished I had been anywhere else but walking to the trench.

For the first few months of World War II, this was the normal procedure whenever the siren sounded a warning of an air raid. Later it was decided that the junior school should sleep in the trenches. By now we were going to bed at half past seven in the evening and quite possibly later.

I know that we slept on the benches, head to toe like sardines! We must have had our pillows with us and certainly blankets to try and make ourselves as comfortable as possible. The members of staff had their mattresses on the duckboards.

On Friday evenings we always had a service in the beautiful Chapel. The senior girls sat near the aisles in each of the rows. If anyone did not feel well, they had to get the attention of a senior girl, so they could be escorted outside. And so on one Friday, I became very dizzy in the middle of the service. One of the seniors helped me out and I was immediately taken to the Sanatorium.

The first words the Sister said to me were, "Where do you sleep?"

"In the trench," I replied.

Where upon I was immediately put to bed and remained in the Sanatorium for a few days, together with several other little girls who also needed a good night's rest. The air raids continued as did the practices. The normal routine of the school had to be flexible. I am sure the staff had many problems to solve in coming up with the best solutions. Eventually a decision was made not to use the trenches for sleeping in. Maybe we would have been taken down there if the school had been in immediate danger. Instead, the staff came up with an alternative idea. The girls in my year all ended up sleeping in one of the junior washrooms downstairs in the House. We had mattresses close together on the floor and we lay head to toe, just as we had done before in the trenches. But this was certainly an improvement compared to our previous sleeping arrangements. At night, the gun barrages could be heard very clearly and we knew there was a number of unexploded bombs in the area of Croxley Green, close to the school.

We were very fortunate, for although we had these disruptions to our normal routines, no bombs fell directly on the school and neither did we ever see any German aircraft.

The beds that remained in the dormitories were all near the wardrobes and away from the windows. Other beds were put end to end through the centre corridors, upstairs and downstairs. In this way we were all able to get a better night's rest.

The typhoid scare must have been in 1940 or 1941. Every girl had to be inoculated against the disease. Obviously we could not all be done at the same time. We were treated in groups and then put to bed in the upstairs corridor. It was a very painful procedure and my arm hurt a great deal. When we rejoined the rest of the school, we had to wear a band on our left arms. The Matron obviously hoped this would offer some kind of protection, but it was not always successful.

When I think of all the organisation that had to be done just in altering the sleeping arrangements, overseeing meals in the Dining Hall, looking after the linen, towels and all our changes of clothes, the House Matrons would have had very challenging and busy times.

Just like at Weybridge, bread became very much our staple food. The long loaves were cut into slices (by machines) in the kitchen, put into large baskets and brought out to the Prefects. To order more bread, we had to put our hands on the table and

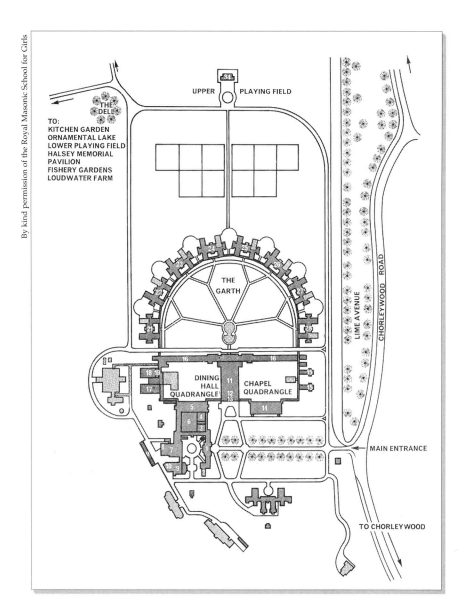

By kind permission of the Royal Masonic School for Girls

A plan of Rickmansworth Masonic Institution for Girls.

Number	House name	Number	House name
21	Ruspini	25	Sussex
22	Zetland	26	Alexandria
23	Moira	27	Atholl
24	Connaught	28	Cumberland

indicate how many slices we wanted by holding up the requisite number of fingers. When we had marmite for tea, we seemed to eat more bread than usual. But we did not have any more butter or margarine to go on it— both were strictly rationed. Most of the time we had to content ourselves with margarine; butter became a treat. In 1940, the weekly ration was only 4oz per person, for margarine and fats 6oz. Each portion was cut into a little pat, about the size of a middle sized pastry cutter.

Looking back at an aerial view of the school, it is obvious that much thought and careful planning had gone into its layout. The eight houses, all identical, were positioned in a semi–circle round an area we called 'The Garth.' We were not allowed to go into another House to visit a friend. Whether or not this rule was introduced just in war time, I do not know. It was a shame though, because I lost contact with several of my little friends from Weybridge. My new friends became the girls who were in the same House and form.

The Weybridge girls still remained separate from the seniors as far as their daily routines were concerned. Prayers were taken by Miss Harrop in the gym, who had her office in the clock tower. By the time April 1940 had arrived, I am writing to Mother:

> Our Brownie uniforms have been brought up from Weybridge AND our gardens are being looked after by the gardeners' children, aren't they kind?

Both the Brownies and the gardens had played a very important part of my life at Weybridge, so I was obviously pleased at having some continuity.

THE ROYAL MASONIC
INSTITUTION FOR GIRLS

152nd
Anniversary Festival

CHAIRMAN:
R.W. Bro. General Sir FRANCIS DAVIES
K.C.B., K.C.M.G., K.C.V.O., V.L.
Deputy Grand Master
Provincial Grand Master for Worcestershire

DISTRIBUTION OF PRIZES
BY
LADY DAVIES, C.B.E.,
AT THE
SENIOR SCHOOL, RICKMANSWORTH PARK
ON
Monday, 6th May, 1940

LEFT and BELOW: the Prize Day Programme. This was the first Prize Day of the war and the first time that girls from Weybridge were present.

I won a prize for drawing and painting, but unlike other years I had to make do with a certificate, while the money was given to the St John War Fund.

LATIN ...	Bro. MAURICE BEACHCROFT
Mona Clinton.	
THE BEST PREFECT ...	Bro. Brig.-General W. H. V. DARELL.
Vera Barker.	
GOOD CONDUCT ...	THE SUPREME COUNCIL 33°
Dorothy Brown.	
SWIMMING ...	Bro. D. C. L. FITZWILLIAMS
Patricia Cadman.	

Junior School Prizes

GENERAL FORM WORK:

FORM A1 ...	Bro. THE EARL OF DONOUGHMORE
Joe Elliott.	
FORM A2 ...	Miss E. M. MATTHEWS
Leslie Denby.	
FORM B1 ...	Mrs. GARBUTT
Joan Williams.	
FORM B2 ...	Bro. B. MARR JOHNSON
Patricia Leopard.	
FORM C ...	Bro. MAURICE BEACHCROFT
Jean Armstrong.	
ARITHMETIC ...	Bro. Major R. L. LOYD
Hermia Clements.	
MUSIC ...	Bro. Sir WILLIAM WYLEY
Beryl Jackson.	
WRITING ...	Bro. LORD HARRIS
Hilda Robson.	
DRAWING AND PAINTING ...	Bro. A. BURNETT BROWN
Barbara Kelland.	
DRILLING ...	Mrs. BURNETT BROWN
Audrey Burgess.	
RECITATION ...	Mrs. MARR JOHNSON
Vera Gardner-Hendren.	
NEEDLEWORK ...	Mrs. HAMILTON
Joyce Hawkins.	
HANDWORK ...	Bro. J. HERBERT BANKES
Margaret Despris.	

God Save the King

6

4.15 p.m. *TEA*

5.15 p.m. *SCHOOL DRILL*

The Pianoforte Pieces will be played by the following girls:

M. Batkin.	P. Hill.	J. Butt.
A. Beech.	B. Hovey.	M. Sandford.
C. Bentham.	M. Henry.	E. Senior.
H. Best.	A. Inns.	R. Senior.
P. Blackwell.	B. Jackson.	J. Senecicle.
S. Bolt.	M. Jackson.	J. Sinclair.
M. Chalk.	Y. Jones.	M. Smith.
D. Cook.	M. Leake.	M. Stokel.
M. Crawford.	R. Low.	L. Thirkarsi.
M. Davies.	C. Lowe.	M. Tye.
M. Edwards.	T. Martin.	M. Vacha.
G. Evans.	J. McLean.	E. Waddington.
O. Evans.	D. Moore.	J. Walker.
R. Evans.	J. Page.	M. Williams.
L. Flare.	P. Pike.	H. Wilson.
B. Forrester.	Y. Prout.	M. Wilson.
M. Goss.	M. Roberts.	J. Witt.
P. Hayward.	M. Russell.	

7

Prize Day was held in early May. Preparations went ahead as usual. On Prize Day in Weybridge, there had always been a concert and entertainment. In spite of the war, 1940 would be no exception. At Weybridge, a tradition had developed of the percussion band from Form B1 performing every year. I had been the conductor for some time and although I was now in the top Form A, Miss Page asked me to continue.

The Assembly Hall at Rickmansworth was one of the most impressive I have ever seen. It seemed vast to me. There were stained glass windows, a balcony and grand pianos either side of the large stage and two portraits of previous Headmistresses. For anyone on their own standing in the middle of the hall, its size was overwhelming.

Music had become such an important part of my school life and there was always an impressive musical arrangement as part of the programme. Eight upright pianos were positioned in a curve and just under the balcony in front of them, was space for the percussion band. Rows of chairs, facing the stage, were placed either side of a central aisle.

Was it Miss Page, my music teacher at Weybridge who had suggested that I lead in and conduct the band? I do not know, but there we were, lined up in the left hand corridor beside the hall. I was at the front by myself and because we were juniors, the Weybridge Headmistress had decided that we should start the Prize Day concert. The little girls who played the drums were immediately behind me and they had to beat to my baton stroke. The time duly arrived and I walked through the double doors, beside the piano on the left of the stage. I remember being aware that the hall was filled with people. The stage was also full and as I turned to walk down the centre, I was very conscious of all the hundreds of pairs of eyes looking at me.

I continued walking forward keeping time, with the little drummers beating the drums at each downward and upward baton stroke. I stopped when we reached the pianos and the members of the percussion band took their places. Everything proceeded smoothly and I am sure that we received a loud round of applause. It was of course the first time that a junior percussion band had performed at Rickmansworth on Prize Day! I was just eleven years old and the memory of those few minutes has stayed with me all these years.

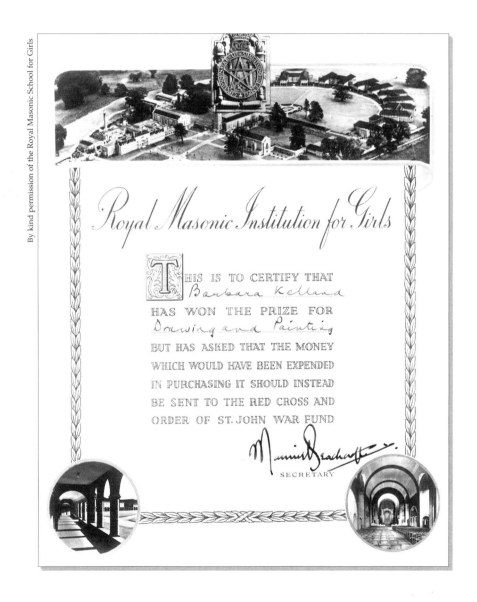

By kind permission of the Royal Masonic School for Girls

Royal Masonic Institution for Girls

THIS IS TO CERTIFY THAT

Barbara Kelland

HAS WON THE PRIZE FOR

Drawing and Painting

BUT HAS ASKED THAT THE MONEY
WHICH WOULD HAVE BEEN EXPENDED
IN PURCHASING IT SHOULD INSTEAD
BE SENT TO THE RED CROSS AND
ORDER OF ST. JOHN WAR FUND

SECRETARY

By kind permission of the Royal Masonic School for Girls

ABOVE: this is the view of the school that I was used to, before the library was built in the centre of 'The Garth' and all the other buildings were added later.

LEFT: the certificate I received for the Drawing and Painting Prize in May 1940.

WORCESTER PARK
1939–40

WORCESTER PARK, 1939-40

What was happening at home after I had returned to school in September 1939? Mother was finding it difficult to obtain work. At the end of October I am writing in capital letters:

> I AM VERY SORRY TO HEAR THAT YOU
> STILL HAVE NO WORK. I DO HOPE YOU
> GET SOME SOON.

The air raids continued and eventually an Anderson shelter was installed in the back garden. Mother's beautiful lawn, which she had taken such care and pains with, had to be dug up. The turf was removed and laid on top of the shelter's corrugated roof. My Grandfather had died in 1938, so the shelter was just large enough for two adults.

We had a long piano stool and it was on this that a makeshift bed was made for me. I do not remember it being very comfortable, but then neither were the benches in the school trench. There was only a small candle to provide light. I know that I had a cover made from an old fur coat, this had been in pieces and Mother had stitched it together again. It would finish its days on a mask that I made at training college in a performance of Milton's

'Comus.' Just like at school, we had our special air raid clothes to keep us warm.

After several months of trying, Mother eventually found a job. Thanks to her expertise in corsetery and her ability to sew, she was employed in a corset factory near the Angel in London. The owner, 'Mr Silhouette' as Mother called him, had escaped from the deteriorating political situation in Austria at some point during the mid 1930s. She had to pass a strict test, demonstrating she could manage an industrial machine, something she had never done before, with 'Mr Silhouette' standing behind her to see that she was a competent worker.

Following the debacle at Dunkirk, which at school we did not really know very much about, the Battle of Britain began. Living so close to London, it was something we could hardly escape from. We knew that the East End and Dockland areas were being very heavily bombed. We could see the red glow to the east, just as we had seen a similar blood red sky when the Crystal Palace had burned down in 1935.

Mother would now came home in the dark, often during an air raid. Whenever this happened, Grandmother and I would already be in the shelter. Mother had to make herself something to eat by candle light and then join us. In the morning she had to get up early and repeat the routine. Air raids sometimes came during the day. With Mother out at work, Grandmother had to manage on her own.

She was a good 'plain cook,' able to make something from very little. For example, instead of a suet rolly polly pudding with currents, 'spotted dick' it was called, she would make a meal with the same suet but add streaky bacon and serve it with cabbage. It cost sixpence. For not only was the food rationed, but there was very little money to go around.

It was my responsibility to look after Grandmother when I was at home. During the height of the Blitz, Mother and I would already be dressed in our air raid clothes, waiting for the alert to sound. I would then go downstairs, get Grandmother out of bed and help her along the garden to the shelter. Mother had her tasks to do and was always last out of the house, once she had made it secure.

I can remember one night very clearly. Mother and I lay on top of the bed, waiting for the sirens. We heard the noise of planes approaching and our local anti–aircraft gun barrage, but we did not move. It was only when the planes were actually overhead that the alert was given. Fortunately the bombs were not dropping near us that night. Perhaps Mother was hoping the planes were ours and we would not have to go down to the shelter. Another time, I went as usual to Grandmother's bedroom to tell her that the siren had sounded and we were all on our way to the shelter, when she turned back to the house.

"Where are you going?" Mother asked.

"I've forgotten my teeth," came the reply. Appearances still had to be maintained whatever the circumstances!

One Sunday the siren went off while Grandmother was making lunch. She ushered Mother and me into the shelter, continued cooking and then with shrapnel falling all around, came along the garden path, carrying our meal on a tray. Raid or no raid, Hitler or no Hitler, Grandmother would not be stopped from cooking. Though it could not have been a very large joint, for the meat ration in 1940 was one shilling and ten pence worth per person.

When I was home it was my task to go and queue at the shops. I became quite used to it. I handed over the ration books, which would be either marked or have the coupons removed. The butcher then cut just the right amount of meat from a very large roll of beef. It was from Argentina and I wonder how many merchant men risked their lives to bring it to us?

Everytime Mother went to work in the morning after a night raid, she had to pick her way very carefully through debris in the road. There was so much damage to property that bricks and rubble were piled high on either side of the railway line to Waterloo Station. The surrounding area suffered a lot of bombing and the Methodists' Church on Waterloo Road, which had played such a big part in the family's life during their time at Mitre Street, had been razed to the ground, only the basement remained.

I became used to seeing shop windows boarded up all over London. At Christmas, Selfridges did not have the usual window displays, which as a little child I thought were magical. I remember being so disappointed that these wonderful scenes would be no more. It was quite usual for shops that were badly damaged, often by fire, to sell the goods at greatly reduced prices. I managed to buy a pair of pale pink quilted slippers with a feather trim and a little heel. I thought these were very 'grown up,' though they did have a distinctive smell!

Because I was away at school most of the time, clothes rationing never really affected me. We were always beautifully turned out in our blue dresses with sparkling white collars, which were changed several times a week. There was always a new dress, winter and summer and a new design each time, which we kept for Committee Days and other special occasions.

Clothes rationing would not have bothered Mother too much either, because she was so expert at sewing. She did not like dressmaking but that did not stop her from running up clothes for herself, Grandmother and me. She was also very good at 'make do and mend,' and at the beginning of the war the LCC had asked her to take classes to show other women how to alter their clothes and how to renovate old clothing so that it appeared like new.

The early war years were a time of sharing, especially when someone was lucky enough to have a special treat. One Christmas, our neighbour had bought a rabbit and then a friend gave him a chicken, and I can still see the rabbit in its roasting dish being carefully given to Mother across the little wall at the front of our house. People helped each other through the difficult times. Everyone made a contribution to the war effort. Mother did a stint at fire watching and learnt how to use a stirrup pump. One of the neighbours was also a fire warden and together they managed a rota system for the neighbourhood.

All the transport systems were still working in our area. We used the Southern Railways to get to Waterloo and then the underground to Baker Street. From there I caught the train to Rickmansworth. As I grew up from a little girl into adolescence, I became used to seeing sandbags around doorways and other entrances. Barrage balloons seemed to fill the entire London sky. Many adults in uniform representing a host of nationalities, walked around the streets, carrying large kit bags. And everyone clutched their gas masks in a container, everyone that is except

ABOVE and RIGHT: Mother's handiwork stands the test of time—her gas mask in its leather case.

Mother. She would not be seen holding a cardboard box. Oh no! She had always liked leather and handbags were one of her weaknesses, along with fashionable hats (she had bought these at Bloomsbury where millinery was one of the subjects). So she found some leather, probably an old bag and made a pattern for the case, to fit the gas mask shape. Then she stitched it together on the good old 'Singer' treadle machine. Now she could go about, carrying a gas mask that at least co–ordinated with her handbags. The cover fitted perfectly and apart from the handle, which has worn away, it is still in remarkably good condition.

During 1940, the air raids at home became more and more frequent and we were using the Anderson shelter in the garden on an almost permanent basis. Of course, when I was away at school, I shared a space with another girl on a mattress on the floor of the washroom. I realise now how very fortunate I was to have had somewhere to lie down, when children of my age in the rest of Europe were being exterminated, dying in battles raging around their homes and being forced to flee their homelands. But of course, all that knowledge would come at a later date.

The only news we received was strictly censored and we either read it in the newspapers, heard it on the wireless, or if I was at the cinema, from the 'Pathé News,' which was always part of the programme.

There were no twenty four hour news channels. Events that were happening elsewhere in the world were not instantly broadcast. It was normal to go to the cinema at whatever time you wanted. The programme was continuous and you were admitted at any point during the showing of the film. Usherettes were always at hand, with their torches, to guide you to a row where there was a vacant seat.

The 'Pathé News' made up part of the programme. This was the only way that we got to see the highlights of sporting events. For example, the boat race, the Grand National and the FA Cup were never shown in their entirety, only the highlights were filmed. We all had to wait until television came into our homes before we could watch national events. To see the Queen's coronation in 1953 live on television, was a very exciting occasion.

At various small cinemas and one at Waterloo Station, the whole programme was made up of news items, and it was here that we could view a fuller version of what was happening in the rest of the world.

Yes, propaganda in war time. Small amounts of footage showed merchant ships battling the forces of nature in the

Atlantic, the 8th Army's successes in north Africa. Or the King and Queen down the East End of London after a bombing raid, Winston Churchill with his 'V' for Victory sign, visiting parts of the capital to boost morale.

Today, we are so accustomed to instant images of world events beamed into our living rooms, that it is strange to think there was a time when everyone had to go about their daily tasks not knowing very much about what was happening elsewhere in the world. The news cinema at Waterloo railway station was by Platform One, high above the entrance. It was a useful place to go and spend some time if you had to wait an hour or so for the next train.

By August, the Nazis had failed to win the battle for control of the skies. For me the memorable high point of that summer was Winston Churchill's resounding speech to the nation, when he praised the role of our brave airmen by declaring, "Never in the field of human conflict was so much owed, by so many, to so few."

But when November came, there were serious food shortages as the impact of the war at sea began to hit home. Carrots ended up taking the place of dried fruit in Christmas puddings and after Christmas Eve no more bananas were imported. Oranges, lemons and onions from Spain were also in short supply. Many years later a colleague of mine, who was born during the war, recalled how he had tried to eat the skin of the very first banana he was given. Because of rationing, that was how unfamiliar some people had become with fruit.

My cousin Doris Woods, who had gone as a supervisor of the London evacuees to Ashwell in Hertfordshire, used to make the most delicious carrot jam, which surprisingly enough did not taste of carrots at all! Unfortunately, I never thought of asking her for the recipe, but it was something that neither her husband Sid nor I, easily forgot eating.

RICKMANSWORTH
1941–45

RICKMANSWORTH, 1941

I wonder whether I would have noticed food rationing quite as
much, if I had been living at home with Mother permanently?
At school, I was used to eating at set times. There was no biscuit
or cake tin to raid if I got hungry. I just had to wait for the next
meal. I had grown used to having a certain amount of sweets each
week, but only on a Sunday. Perhaps that was why my early
letters from Rickmansworth contained so many references to
food. I suppose what we ate was rather bland.

When we did have a change, it was something to write home
about. The following extracts are taken from letters written
during the early war years:

> February, 1941.
> Have you heard from Sister yet? I have to have
> some sort of ginger with rhubarb in it and it's
> horrid. I have lost 2lbs 6oz, so now I weigh 5st
> 3lbs 6ozs instead of 5st 5lbs 12oz. (I was
> constantly losing weight).
>
> Today (Saturday) we had something that
> nobody can get—now guess? ONIONS what a

surprise! I'm cross, I can't have suet pudding and that means I can't have treacle. What a shame, so I have to have chocolate blancmange and you know I much I like it, URR!! Now another thing—marmalade for breakfast yesterday and rice and jam for dinner.

The other day we had cheese and celery for tea and the piece of cheese we all had was really tiny. Please excuse my writing. I expect you have noticed that further back in my letter I said Saturday. Well, I am writing this on Saturday so goodbye 'till tomorrow when I will continue.

Hello Mummy, it is Sunday now and we have just come back from dinner. We had pork, potatoes and cabbage and for afters, batter pudding and treacle.

Batter pudding and treacle was often on the menu and as every Masonic school girl knew, it was called bath mat! That week for some reason, seemed to be a good week for food. I have no recollection of being allowed to go to Rickmansworth during the early war years. Later when we were older yes, but not in 1941. However, in May that year I wrote:

I went down to the village on Monday morning with some of the other girls. I tried to get more sweets and I got three packets of wine gums and a bar of chocolate, so I spent five pence (this seems very cheap!) We had oranges for dinner on Thursday. (The oranges of course would have been the pudding).

May, 1941.

As I am writing this letter, I am sucking my last sweet (there it goes) now I can't have anymore till next Sunday. We are allowed two penny worth of sweets, but we only get nine for two penny worth.

February, 1942.

I am glad you had a nice time out with Uncle Jack (he was my Godfather). Yes, you did make my mouth water when you told me you had turkey. But the other day we had corned beef and pickles and another time we had salmon mould for dinner.

Someone was trying to make our meals interesting, for I am sure it was quite a headache working out the menu from the rations they were allocated.

September 20, 1942.

My dear Mummy,

I was so pleased to get your letter and parcel. It cheered me up, for I am in the San now as I write this to you, but I hope to go back tomorrow. I told you that Smith (House Matron) would send me to the San and it made me feel homesick, but never mind. I hope when this reaches you, you will have settled down at your new little home at which you are to spend a week. I do hope you will enjoy yourself. I do wish that I could be with you but still it can't be—never mind.

It has been very lonely up here where I am, because I am in a ward all by myself in one little bed with two other people in different wards, who are also by themselves. We are all upstairs, but now we have a wireless so it's not so bad after all. It is something to amuse our minds. I am back at school as you can see, as I am writing my letter in ink.

I thought of you on Saturday and wasn't it a lovely day for you to travel. I do hope you have a nice time there.

We have got a new mistress in our House. Her name is Miss Keyes. She is quite nice but you never know what she will turn out like.

Hardly any of us are able to have sweets this week as Miss Smith says that we have had our ration for this week, so we have to go without. But do you know we can only have two penny worth instead of ¼lb.

We have just been weighed again and I weigh 6st 9lbs 12oz. It is raining here today and I do hope that it does not rain all this week because it will be horrible for you.

Well, this is all for now, all my love and kisses, from your little daughter,
Barbara.

I mention this letter because I am still talking about the sweet ration, not surprising as Sunday was sweet day, so it was very much on my mind. I do not recall being in the Sanatorium, but we were always being looked after whatever our ailments. I remember that Mother had to spend time at a rest home and this was probably the time. Miss Stella Keyes replaced Miss Wright— she was a jolly person and I got on well with her, but more of that later.

> November, 1942.
> I am longing for Christmas this year aren't you?
> Have you had my sweet coupons yet?
>
> Because Miss Fryer said that they were going to send them home to our parents, so I was wondering whether you have got them, also our ORANGE books for we are able to have oranges—those up to eighteen years of age.

This last sentence was news to me and shows how scarce and precious oranges were as they had to be shipped to this country from warmer areas, but again at what cost to men's lives? It was just as well we did not know what sacrifices had been made. We never saw instant images of torpedoed merchant ships and consequent loss of life. Oranges of course are a valuable source of vitamin C, but we also discovered another source, rose hips. In a letter written in 1943–44, I mention this:

> It's just an awful day today, teeming with rain and so cold that we have had to put on our serge dresses. What a life! Also this morning, another girl and myself were going hip picking, but as it is still raining we can't go out.

Where did we go rose hip picking? It would have been somewhere in the vicinity of the school but I have no recollection.

I am continuing to lose weight in 1943:

> We have just been weighed and I weigh 6st
> 11lbs 10oz. I have lost 2lbs 11oz. Last time I was
> 7st 0lbs 5oz, so I must eat a lot more and that I
> will, so don't worry.

Perhaps by now I had moved up nearer the end of the dining
table where the senior girls sat and therefore had a little more
food to eat, for in a letter in June, 1941 I wrote:

> Somebody in our Common Room has chocolate
> finger biscuits, a few small cakes, a small swiss
> roll and a good lot of sweets. I can only wish I
> could have all those things when you come to
> visit me. You know I told you we ate so much
> bread, well it was because we don't get enough
> to eat at dinner. You see the seniors at the end of
> the table have a lot on their plates and then have
> another helping, while us poor little things in
> the middle half starve and we have a long time
> to wait till tea time and at supper we only have
> thin biscuits, so you see we are quite hungry.

We had made ourselves a chart, which we stuck in our lockers
and kept an account of the slices of bread we were eating at every
meal. Sometimes I had recorded ten slices! It must have been
mostly dry bread, for if there was any jam for tea then there was
no cake and if there was cake, as there was on Committee Day,
there was no jam. Marmite days were looked forward to. Each
table had a large jar of the black savoury spread and by the end of
the meal (half an hour) we had eaten it all—Marmite is oddly
addictive. We had margarine and butter that was cut into little
pats about the size of a medium pastry cutter. These were evenly

distributed and had to last us the meal no matter how many pieces of bread we ate. We knew that there was no point in, "asking for more." Whether we liked it or not, we had to eat whatever food was served. These rules applied just as they had done at Weybridge and only if a particular food made us ill or we had an allergic reaction, were we exempt from eating it.

I think those of us in Zetland have always remembered the struggle one of our friends Dawn had with the tapioca pudding, our name for it of frogs spawn I am sure did not help! As a junior she had no chance of asking for the smallest serving possible, so she had to sit there facing this plate of tapioca trying to swallow it, even the large glasses of water did little to disguise the taste. Her only reprieve came when she was made a Prefect and could have some say in how much she wanted to eat—or not! We had our allocation of milk each day and there was always another glass for supper and I remember oat cakes or a bun or biscuits. Supper was taken in our own House and served in the Common Room.

And did we go to the dentist? Yes, we certainly did. At Weybridge I can remember Miss Page taking me with another girl to have a filling. The drill made an horrendous noise. At Rickmansworth, in a letter to Mother, I wrote that Dawn had to go to the dentist, but to my great relief I did not.

Matron weighed us in the linen room and it was there that we went if we received a parcel from home, which had to be opened in her presence. It was also the place where the sweets were handed out. In addition to Miss Iris Wade, each House also had its own Matron and I am sure there was plenty for them to do. Apart from all the linen and bedding, there were special bath towels, linen comb bags that hung on hooks in the bathroom, in which we all kept our brushes and combs. We had several sets of pyjamas. Then there were the underclothes, stockings, socks, all in different sizes.

We had winter coats, summer blazers, velour and Panama hats, not to mention all our pairs of shoes and again special shoes for Committee Day. And we always wore white collars—these had press studs in three places and had to match the press studs in the neck of the dresses! We changed them regularly throughout the week.

We were always immaculately presented with never a hair out of place. It was simply not allowed! If your hair touched your white collar then it had to be cut or tied in bunches with a rubber band. If it was longer, then it had to be plaits, tied with a ribbon. Those of us with short hair used to perfect the art of making beautiful butterfly bows, in lovely blue ribbons for the girls with plaits. It became quite a skill and we were very proud of our ability to tie them correctly.

All the clothes were marked with a number. As I was in Zetland House my possessions were marked on tape with a Z35. Then last but not least, there were the white counterpanes for our beds. Many of these had floral borders. It was quite something to see all the rows of beds beautifully made and covered. We took such pride in their appearance, we even did hospital corners! To this day I have counterpanes and I do not like the modern fashion of just leaving the bed with a duvet showing. Years of training in early life are hard to erase!

In my first official year at Rickmansworth (1940–41), there was an inter-house singing competition. This of course gave all the girls something to work for and provided an interest. We would practice regularly with Miss Smith, our Matron, playing the piano and with me as the conductor. Yes, I might have been in the first year, but everyone still wanted me to conduct the singing, for they had been in the Assembly Hall in May 1940 when I had walked up the centre aisle conducting the percussion band.

I can clearly recall that when the school was informed at the end of prayers, that there would be a singing competition, all the girls in Zetland House looked towards me. I do not remember if we won and I expect Miss Maiden would have been the main judge. She was our singing teacher and I am sure all my friends still recall her teaching us to breath, hold ourselves correctly and sing the right notes. I never took part in the competition, as I was not chosen for the choir. But how I longed to sit in the stalls of our lovely Chapel! I am sure Mother would have been so pleased because she had such a good soprano voice. I had to wait until I got to training college, but it was not quite the same as singing in the Masonic school choir.

Committee Day was the third Thursday in each month. I realise now that it was the House Committee which met, obviously those Freemasons who were responsible for running the school. On these occasions there was always a very large slice of fruit cake at the end of the table, next to the Prefect. When we had duly eaten our bread and butter or margarine, we had to talk quietly (there were over 400 girls, so that was quite an achievement), and wait for the Committee members to come into the dining room and cut the cake.

They did not make it to all the tables but we used to guess which ones the gentlemen of the committee would go to. We knew it would be where the pretty eighteen year olds sat—after all they were young women in the bloom of youth and we were always right! I say we, because I was surrounded by a lot of girls my own age. Why there were so many of us, in the same House I do not know. There were eight in the Upper V, four in the Lower V and commercial class and four in the year below us, so we formed quite a formidable group and it was no wonder we were often in trouble.

Our House Mistress, Miss Margaret Vickridge had her hands full, for there was always someone who would think up naughty things to do.

Early in the war, we decided that when the Prefects spoke to us we would respond with the Nazi salute, and when we answered, we would salute with our right hand above our eyebrows, like members of the British armed forces. Clearly Miss Vickridge could not allow that to go on. Upstairs to Dormitory Three we all went. By this time the beds had been moved to the end of the dormitory, nearest the wardrobes and away from the windows, leaving a large space. Miss Vickridge, 'Vic' as we called her, told us to spread out along the wall and face it.

"Now raise your right arms!"

So there we stood all making the Nazi salute and we had to stay like that until Vic told us we could lower our arms. After a while Dawn who a tall girl and whose arm could reach the wall, obviously began to tire. She supported her hand on the wall.

"Hitler wouldn't think much of that Dawn!" said Vic.

I am sure she was smiling when she uttered these words and needless to say she had put paid to our little scheme. We were twelve years old and had no idea anymore than the rest of the country did, what despicable crimes were being perpetrated against people in the rest of Europe, suffering under Nazi occupation.

It was about this time that the factory where Mother was working had to close down. I do not think I ever knew the reasons why and maybe Mother did not either. Perhaps it proved too difficult to get the right fabrics that were needed or the sales were affected, (we did have clothes rationing) or maybe the factory had been damaged in the Blitz. Whatever the reason, Mother found herself out of work again. Once more, she had to start looking for some kind of a job. On July 6, 1941, I wrote to Mother:

> I should absolutely hate, hate!!! you to go on a
> milk round, it would be terrible.

I think this comment shows just how completely out of touch I was with the normal routine of a household. Where would people have been without the daily delivery of milk to their door steps? There was no long life milk or supermarkets to supply it. The deliveries were essential for everyone. The milkmen were no doubt being called up for active service in the forces. This was happening in all the areas when men had been employed and women were replacing them. Women worked in the factories and on the railways, they also drove lorries and ambulances. Many of them if they were married, would not continue working once the war ended. But while their jobs lasted, they were having an entirely new set of experiences. This was to have quite a dramatic effect on the way they came to view the kind of work their husbands had been doing.

And so it was that one day, Mother saw an advertisement in a national newspaper, 'Women Wanted for Railway Porters.' She knew she was strong and probably thought she was more than capable of pushing a trolley. When she went for her interview, it became apparent that Mother would be better employed in other areas and not on the uniform staff. So she started work in an office. By November 1941, she was writing to me:

> Don't faint! But I'm on another different job. Yes! I'm just like a football from one office to another. I am again in the ARP office—that means Air Raid Prevention. I am learning all about the Roster, that means fixing 700 men on fire watch every night. We take off the names from large sheets, five in all and twenty four sheets have to be run off, so we put them on 'jelly.' You would love to do it. It is so interesting. It is an old custom of printing. You can print onto clean paper, more than one hundred men's names in two minutes.
>
> I hope I'm here for good now, I simply hated the job I was in last week and told Mr C so. In fact,

if he had refused to move me, I had intended writing to London Bridge for a transfer back to the uniform staff. There is only another girl (junior school teacher 'till her marriage), in the room with me. She is showing me what to do. We have a new electric fire installed and it's lovely and warm—I was frozen all last week in the other office—we have no bosses over us and only take orders from one man who is right over in the staff office.

With the recruitment of so many women as part of the war effort, the government realised it needed to look after their welfare. This was how Mother found an opening on what was then called the Southern and South Eastern Railways. She was promoted to Welfare Officer, at the Nine Elms depot, Vauxhall. She visited the women at home if they had not reported for work, looked into their working conditions and helped with any problems they might have had. After the years of uncertainty at the beginning of the war, Mother now had an office job. I found the following little note written on a scrap of paper in pencil—obviously recording areas to be looked into:

> Can wood be supplied for lobby in A shed?
> More pegs for clothes, as clothes have to be left anywhere for new staff. A shed and small lobby.
> Lavatories in A shed and Hydraulic shed, very much fouled seat and floor—notices needed.
> No permit for milk—would use canteen if they (women) had services. Canteen would not allow a sandwich to be sold as they were wanted for the men. Can't get served in the cafe because of the large crowd.
> Key to be left in Albert Weigh Bridge.

Small and insignificant as the above items might seem now, they would have been important to the women at the time. They needed to have someone they could turn to, who would express their grievances and generally try to improve things. Mother always smiled at the reception she once received on going to the home of a woman who had been absent from work. A small girl opened the flat door and announced, "She's gorn to the 'ospital wiv 'er chest."

Mother also discovered that many of the women had begun to realise some of the work their husbands had been doing, was not quite as strenuous and tiring as the men used to make out! I think this remained true in a lot of areas. This started to make them think. And of course, running the home and looking after children without the appliances and facilities that are available today, was no easy task and was often far more demanding than some of the men's work!

The government's campaign to encourage women to contribute to the war effort was launched with the help of posters. One I remember well, was of a woman standing in overalls with arms outstretched, aircraft overhead and behind her, a factory on one side and tanks on the other, with the caption reading:

> Women of Britain
> Come into THE FACTORIES
> Male trainees age 41 and 42, £3.0.6 per week
> Female trainees £1.18.0 per week

Of course it was not just in the factories where they were needed. The men (under forty) were being called up from the farming communities and women were desperately required to fill these places. There were posters depicting women in the 'Land Army' as it was called, but it was very, very physical work and a lot of them found it exhausting. Another poster called for us to, 'Dig for Victory,' which had a large spade with a foot on the front of it, encouraging us to dig up our lawns and grow vegetables. The number of allotments increased during this time, as everyone made an effort to grow more food. Posters telling us about the dangers of gossip were put in prominent places. 'Careless Talk Costs Lives,' and, 'Be Like Your Dad—Keep Mum,' reminded us not to chatter to friends on trains, trams, the underground, buses or anywhere else for that matter—no one knew where the enemy was listening. It would have been so easy, especially for parents in the armed forces with children, to innocently make some comment referring to their ship or regiment that if overheard, might have divulged sensitive information to the enemy. By the autumn term of 1941, I wrote to Mother:

> Well, now Mummy do you think that you could send me some more things. I know I am being an awful nuisance, but wait until you hear what we are doing in our Common Room. You know we are always up to pranks and doing different things. We are making a blanket, but we have decided to make two blankets, also you will never guess, well, we are having a bazaar.

> Yes, we are all having different stalls and making all different things. Granny (nickname for Pat) and I are having a stall with Christmas cards and brooches. We have got a few Christmas cards and a few brooches but we have got a raffle and nothing for that, so I am wondering if you would please send me a doll. She is celluloid and in my cupboard, with no clothes on, only a pixie hat.

Also a little wooden thing, you know a sewing doll with a few pins stuck in the top and you go round and round with wool and it comes out a long snaky thing. Please, also some more material and some more wool if you can get any. Also, can you get black mending wool as Granny and I want to make little pompon cats as brooches. Also in my little room, there are some black stockings and black velvet. Would you be a dear and send them to me?

Oh! yes and if you find any felt any little bits even if they are only very small. We can make do with them, also some safety pins any kind as many as you can please Mummy, for we are going to sell them and the money we are going to give to the merchant navy and we are going to ask Vic that with the money, she will buy the men cigarettes.

I have said a lot about that haven't I? Oh! do you know I can scull in swimming and Miss Elliot said I was the best in the form. (Miss Elliot was our special swimming teacher and swimming was to become one of my favourite lessons).

Well here's all for now. Lots of love from your little daughter,
Barbara.

In 1942, the bazaar was our contribution to the war effort. We worked very hard to make it a success, spurred on without a doubt because Vic bless her, had offered to double whatever money we raised. Now, that is what I call an incentive!

There were also fund raising efforts in the school by the Guides and other groups. I know that we knitted garments for the sailors—or at least attempted to I should say. The school had adopted two merchant ships and one of the photographs hung on the wall underneath the clock in Zetland senior Common Room. This would have been either 'The Ocean Courier' or 'The Trevilley.' Sadly, it seems that 'The Trevilley' was lost as a result of enemy action later in the war.

By June, there was quite a lot of excitement at school. My letter at the end of May tells Mother that:

> The London Symphony Orchestra is coming on Sunday, June 7, and we all thought we would not be able to go, but Miss Fryer said that the Music Society could go as far down as the 3rd Form. So you can imagine how glad we were.

The next letter on June 7, 1942 was written, as always sometime during Sunday, probably after lunch at midday:

> Oh Mummy, I am so excited and don't know what to do—tonight I'm going to bed at ten o'clock. You see, I am going to the concert. I am just longing, next week, I will tell you all about it. The hall looks lovely. All the platform is decorated with flowers.

> June 14, 1942.
> I had a lovely time on Sunday. I have given myself a task if I am going to tell you all about

the concert, so I decided to start to write on Thursday night to get it finished. First of all, we went over at twenty to eight and sat down in our places on the balcony, there was a great clatter of excitement and most of the people had arrived.

At last the orchestra came in, then the leader. We all clapped him, then the conductor, Keith Douglas. He was tall and oh! such a lovely conductor. I should think that nearly all the girls fell in love with him—not really though!

It was the most wonderful thing I ever saw, especially when Moiseiwitsch came and played the piano, it was lovely. I was so fascinated that I could just sit and stare, his hands were lovely, up and down. Then we had the interval and they played another piece, which lasted all the rest of the time. It finished at ten past ten.

We were quite tired when we got back to the House and Vic gave us two more biscuits each. I will send you the programmes so you will be able to see something of what it was like, if you read what it says under all the headings. It tells you about the piece and what all the different instruments do and when they come in.

The recollections of that evening have remained with me always. I can still remember Moiseiwitsch sitting at the beautiful grand piano and Keith Douglas on a podium in front of the platform, surrounded by flowers and the tails of his dress coat swinging from side to side. Because I had been a conductor in my own little way, I was utterly entranced by him, and as Moiseiwitsch played the piano I was enraptured by his hands. It was an evening never to be forgotten. Though for once I do not seem to have remembered that we had extra biscuits. But I do recall being told to go to bed very quietly and not wake any of the other girls in the dormitory.

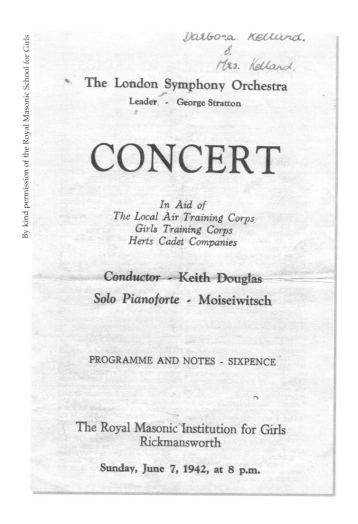

By kind permission of the Royal Masonic School for Girls

Barbara Kelland.
&
Mrs. Kelland.

The London Symphony Orchestra

Leader - George Stratton

CONCERT

In Aid of
The Local Air Training Corps
Girls Training Corps
Herts Cadet Companies

Conductor - Keith Douglas

Solo Pianoforte - Moiseiwitsch

PROGRAMME AND NOTES - SIXPENCE

The Royal Masonic Institution for Girls
Rickmansworth

Sunday, June 7, 1942, at 8 p.m.

The Programme cover for the June 1942 concert, with the names of war time beneficiaries.

Apart from our little cat at home, I grew up without the company of animals. It would have been impractical to say the least for us to have had any pets, particularly during the war. But Miss Vickridge had a small terrier whose name was Sam. The girls in the House paid him a lot of attention, but I was never particularly drawn to the little creature—unlike Tris, who was always playing with him and wanted to train so much as a vet when she left school.

Some people have a natural empathy with animals and Tris was certainly one of them. I mention Sam now because of an episode I wrote about to Mother. As there is no date on the letter, I am guessing that it was sometime between 1941–42, because Miss Smith was still the House Matron. Here is what I wrote:

> This morning in the walk, Brenda found a dead baby fox. It happened while we were in Chapel. Sam had killed the fox by biting it in the neck. When Miss Vickridge came back, Sam was sitting very innocently in Miss Vickridge's room. Brenda found the fox under some bushes and at first she thought it was a rabbit, but she picked it up by its back legs and carried it up to the House. We put it in the Senior Common Room where they gave it to Miss Vickridge. Luckily Sam was not there. She laid it on a piece of paper and we asked Miss Butcher to come and see it. She is the biology mistress, then Miss Bates came, also Miss Blackledge and Miss Smith. In the end, we decided to have it stuffed.

Whether we did or not I cannot recall, but the catching of the fox obviously caused a lot of commotion and discussion. I write elsewhere in reply to Mother's letter that, 'No, we have decided not to stuff all the foxes that Sam kills!'

But in addition to Sam there were also two cats. If I had not mentioned them twice in my letters, I would have said that the only animal at school was Sam the dog. Here are the extracts in June of the same year:

> Two of our ginger cats have had kittens, Huxley and Scamp. Scamp had her kittens in our House on a chair in the study, three of them have been drowned and old Scamp was out looking for them down by the tennis courts, poor thing.

Mother had made some comment about the kittens in her next letter, and it had obviously made an impression on me, for I am replying on June 8:

> Yes, they have left two kittens for Scamp, it is a shame why they should take them away. I would have loved to have a baby kitten. I saw them when they were two days old.

And what about the bluebell wood? The memory of a bluebell wood has always stayed with me, carpets of blue beneath the trees, which spread out forever. But where was it? And when did we go to find it? Was it on one of the routine Sunday walks? Fortunately the following letter tells me.

I was so pleased to read it, for I knew that at sometime during my time at Rickmansworth we had discovered the wood. The letter is dated June 1, but unfortunately there is no year and the stamp has not been franked. Looking at the writing and the note paper, I think it would have been 1941.

> It is lovely because we are having our half term holiday now, Friday, Saturday, Sunday and

Monday. On Saturday Miss Wright (one of the Weybridge staff, and Brown Owl in my Weybridge photograph with Miss Vaughan), came into the Common Room and asked if anyone would like to go and pick some bluebells.

Of course we all went, so we put on our Panama hats and gloves, got in partners and as we went up the Garth everybody else was staring at us. Then we went out of the school gates and down the Valley Road. After quite a good walk, we came to a place called the 'chump,' where we rushed into it because there were the bluebells and then I started picking furiously, pulling up four together, after that we walked straight on. Then we came to a log, where the little ones sat down to rest. After that we went on our way and got lost but managed to get back to school in time. Miss Wright said we walked about four or five miles and it was glorious!

The little ones I mentioned would probably have been the Weybridge girls, but one big surprise for me re–reading the letter was the fact that we wore gloves! I have always liked them, but I had not realised we put them on for walks.

Perhaps that was when my love of gloves first began, for I still wear them, even in summer. I have a selection of wrist length, coloured cotton ones. Then I have three quarter length ones, that reach just below the elbow. And at the back of my glove and scarf drawer, I have a pair of long black suede and pale pink leather gloves, that fit over the elbow and half way up to the top of the arm.

I continued to take music as an extra subject. There were pianos in many areas of the school. The two large music rooms at one end of the classroom corridor, opposite the gym and swimming pool, both had cubicles, each one containing an upright piano, similar to Weybridge. In the Assembly Hall, not only were there two grand pianos, but also there were more upright ones, which were placed in a semi–circle under the balcony when concerts were performed on Committee and Prize Days. There was another grand piano in the Dining Hall for when we sang grace at the beginning and end of every meal. Each Senior Common Room in the Houses also had an upright piano. We went into the Hall to the sound of the piano and were led out of assembly to music. I continued practising the piano, a letter dated May 1949 said:

> Yes, the piano came off all right. It was Prize
> Day and I was playing solo.

I am sure if it had been solo, I would have had more to say than just one line! However, here is my account of my music exam in November 1941. It was the Associated Board of the Royal School of Music, London, Grade IV (Lower):

> I had my exam on Wednesday morning. I was
> first and the man's name was Sir Percy Walls,
> and he was very nice. First of all, he asked me
> when I went in if I was cold or warm, evidently
> I was warm because I had warmed myself by
> Miss Hudson's fire (shades here of fuel
> shortages during war time).

> I sat down and he asked me for some scales and
> arpeggios, then some sight reading. It was fairly
> hard, but I managed to struggle through. Then

he asked me to do some oral tests, and I had to sing the top note then the bottom and middle one.

After that he said I could play my pieces. I started and I only made one mistake and that was at the end and in my other two pieces I only made one mistake and that was also at the end. So I don't think I did too badly.

I passed the exam and have a beautiful certificate that I still treasure even after all these years. And music of course, made up such a large part in our Chapel services. Miss Joyce Brown, who was my piano teacher, also played and taught the organ and it was in the Chapel listening to her rendering of Bach's 'Toccata and Fugue in B Flat Minor,' and 'Sheep May Safely Graze,' that remain my main memories—apart from the fact that I also wanted to sing in the choir!

Unfortunately, by the time I reached my Higher Grade and failed it, I decided not to take music anymore. Oh yes, I remember Miss Brown talking to me for such a long time, as she tried to change my mind, and persuade me to continue.

But adolescent girls are often very obstinate and I refused. I have since thought a lot about that decision—which I admit was a wrong one. I liked playing the piano but I was beset with anxiety if I made just one wrong note—the impact of Wigmore Hall in 1939 I wonder? Whatever the reason, I did not alter my decision. If only someone had said, "All right Barbara, we won't enter you for the exam, but learn to play so that you enjoy it," I would have been delighted—and yes who knows, I might have eventually passed another exam!

Zetland House had a reputation for winning the inter-house lacrosse cup and from our earliest years in the House we—well I did anyway—longed to play lacrosse. As I have mentioned, there was a large number of us in Zetland, all about the same age, and consequently when we became old enough (and good enough of course), we were chosen to represent the school in the first team. Here is an extract from a letter of November 29, 1942:

> Yesterday we had good luck with all the matches that we played. The lacrosse team won 22 : 0. I did feel sorry for the other school for they were not very good at all and they were a Convent. The other match was a hockey match against some (well most), of the county team players. There were only about three who were not and WE WON 6 : 4.
>
> I think the school was jolly good and we are jolly good at all games. I think we have only lost two games this term and nearly every half holiday we have played a match.

Because so many of us from Zetland played Lacrosse and most of us were good at sports, Jackie and June out shone the rest of us—we very often made up the full school team. We had of course Gwen who was Victrix Ludorum and June (who still continued to play Lacrosse all her adult life) as examples, and since they were senior girls in the House, it was just a natural progression that we wished to emulate them. Yes, we might have eaten a lot of bread at meal times, but we played a lot of sports too!

While we were rushing about on the playing fields of Rickmansworth, World War II was continuing with increasing ferocity in north Africa. The battles against the German Afrika Korps under the command of Field Marshal Rommel, were not going well and the 8th Army had suffered many defeats. Coupled with the earlier setback at Dunkirk, morale was not high.

Then Winston Churchill changed the north African command and appointed General Montgomery. By October–November 1942 the situation had changed. The British army won a huge victory at El Alamein. So important was this breakthrough not only for the besieged 8th Army but for the morale of the British people, that Churchill ordered the church bells to be rung.

Since the start of the war in September 1939, the government decreed that the ringing of the bells would be the signal across Britain that the Nazi invasion of our island had begun—an event which everyone believed was going to happen at some point.

I do not recall the bells though, just a mention in the only letter I still have from Mother. Here is a small reference, the date is November 18, 1942:

> Yes! I did hear a faint 'bell' on Sunday. I believe it was from St Mary's Cuddington. I am glad you enjoyed Sunday so much, it was certainly a lovely day for many people all over the country.
>
> Wait 'till the Peace Bells ring out and we have peace again.

Obviously from Mother's comments, the school must have celebrated the day in a special way, no doubt with a service of thanksgiving in our beautiful Chapel. Whatever it was, I obviously found it memorable enough to mention in my letters to her.

I discovered the following account that Mother had kept from

a newspaper clipping of the time, which describes the impact of
the occasion very well:

> Suddenly the bells of victory were ringing out
> along the length and breadth of the land. From
> the towers of the great cathedrals they sounded
> the nation's joy at the news from Egypt. It was
> the first time they had been rung since the threat
> of German invasion in 1940. The whole world
> heard Britain rejoicing through the BBC
> Overseas Service. After a peal rang out from the
> bomb shattered Coventry Cathedral where the
> spire and bell tower were still standing, an
> announcer asked, "Did you hear the bells in
> occupied Europe? Did you hear them in
> Germany?"

In London, St Paul's Cathedral led the chorus of celebration
together with what remained of the undamaged City churches.
Many of the ringers were volunteers from the services. Some of
the churches joining in had also been built by Wren after the first
Great Fire of London in 1666. Only this time, following the Blitz
of 1940, far fewer still stood intact.

It is very hard, if not impossible for anyone born during or
after the war, to have the slightest conception of what life was like
in Germany or the rest of Europe in 1942. In fact, most of us living
in Britain at the time, could not have imagined being occupied by
another country. The population as a whole was unaware of the
deprivation suffered by people across the continent, and the daily
risks willingly undertaken by those who fought against the
occupying powers.

Anyone caught with a wireless set and listening to a British
broadcast would have been shot. The life expectancy of a wireless
operator working in the resistance movement was very short,

something like three weeks. But I was to learn more about these things later in my life. Occupied Europe stretched a long way in 1942, from Norway in the north west to Greece in the south east and the Nazi armies were attacking Russia.

By now members of my family had been called up to fight and contribute to the war effort. Mother's brother, Uncle Frank was drafted into the army. Roderick the eldest cousin also went into the army and later near the end of the war, was involved in the Italian campaign. Mavis still worked at the dockyards in Plymouth. Ivor had joined the Royal Navy and was on the battle-ship HMS Repulse. In 1942, he was transferred to one of the escort ships, which accompanied the Russian convoys operating between the Clyde and Murmansk in Northern Russia. And Aileen worked at the Admiralty.

In September 1941, I wrote to Mother asking her if she knew which regiment Uncle Frank was in. I do not think I got a reply. Frank was the artist in the family. He had inherited his ability from his father and who knows how far back his talent went.

But Frank's time in the army was to be cut short. One evening, a high ranking officer visited Uncle's regiment, which was putting on some kind of evening entertainment. Frank was responsible for all the artwork on the menus and when the visiting officer saw the quality and high standard of his designs, he immediately asked for the name of the man responsible.

The following day, Frank was summoned by his commander and the next thing he knew, he was dispatched to a section at Bletchley Park (the British government's secret code breaking establishment), where he spent the duration of the war.

Frank signed the Official Secrets Act and never discussed in any detail what he got up to between 1939-45. But later, from time to time, he did give us little hints. He was in a section that forged important documents for agents and people in the resistance movements.

I remember him telling me how one of his colleagues had been busy all morning reproducing a German food coupon. He had faithfully finished the whole thing, complete with a small but visible black spot in one of the corners. Then he suddenly moved the document and the black spot fell off—it had never been a part of the original! But this little incident was an indication of the high level of precision their work required. Frank used to practice the signatures of German officers, making sure his hand flowed smoothly, so there was no stopping and starting, because this would have caused little blots of ink, which could have been detected when the signature was magnified and displayed on a screen.

He once said that his eyesight had deteriorated during this time as he had to use such a powerful magnifying glass and the work was so exacting. He died not so long ago aged ninety two, never divulging anybody's name or the exact nature of the materials he had been asked to forge.

Even though I had such little contact with Uncle Frank, I was very proud of his contribution to the war effort and particularly the help his work must have provided to the people who were operating in the resistance movements on the continent.

Mother's job as a Welfare Officer, meant she was moving between the depots in the Old Kent Road and Nine Elms in Vauxhall. Safe as I was at Rickmansworth and being well looked after, I really did not have any idea of how Mother was coping with the effects of the war on her life.

The daily grind of eking out the food and clothing rations (these were coupons we had to save up, in order to have enough to buy the items we needed), was very hard. Although Mother was brilliant at turning her hand to anything that required making, she still had to buy clothes for herself and Grandmother.

Day to day living was dreary. All around us in the suburbs were constant reminders of the scars left behind by Hitler's bombs—shored up ends of houses, piles of rubble, (what was left of bombed houses and business premises), barrage balloons everywhere in the sky above London, sand bags and air raid shelters in the centre of the streets. Eros boarded up in Leicester Square, did look strange and the danger of air raids either during the day or night was ever present.

I am again writing to Mother about the raids. Fortunately, because of where we were in Rickmansworth, we did not have to go into the trenches every time the air raid siren sounded. I often became worried if Mother's weekly letter had not arrived at school on the day expected, usually a Wednesday. There are many little references to this in my replies to her.

One day in March I wrote:

> I do hope that you are all right after the raid on Wednesday. We heard the guns from here and they sounded very heavy, as much as we could see, for we looked out of the dormitory windows in the first raid.

In another letter, later in the year, I said:

> I was so pleased to get your letter and to know that you are all right after the raid. I am glad that you met Uncle Jack (my Godfather) after all on Monday. I hope you had a nice time (fancy hoping that, I know you always do).

> Yes, we had the air raid and lots of guns, they must have been London guns. I heard that the barrage was very heavy. Some of the girls had a great deal of difficulty in getting here, as the Baker Street line had a bomb on it. The first person who came back on Monday afternoon, came at 3:00 pm.

In the morning we went to the pictures to see 'The Great Mr Handel.' It was good and all in colour. When we came back it was time for dinner so that passed the morning and we only had to wait for the rest to come in the afternoon.

Yes, bombs on the railway line or anywhere else for that matter, caused disruption to the daily routine. Sometimes they landed and did not explode. Then whole areas were cordoned off and brave men called in to defuse and make them safe.

Uncle Jack was often in London on business. Like my Father, he also worked for the British Thompson Houston Company. Whenever he had any spare time he would often take Mother out for a meal. Despite the war, hotels, restaurants and cafes were still open for business. On one such occasion, I happened to be at home during the holidays.

It was winter time and everywhere was blacked out. Because of this, I had no idea where we were going in the taxi. We had of course caught the train from Worcester Park and met Uncle at the hotel where he was staying. Earlier in the war, he had a very lucky escape while sleeping at the Charing Cross Hotel. He awoke one morning, to find half the wall in the room opposite, demolished during an air raid on the nearby station.

Driving through London in the dark was very strange. This was a great treat for me, because we usually only ever travelled on the Underground. I have since realised that we were heading for the Lyons Corner House Brasserie at Marble Arch. The brasserie at that time was like an open courtyard with an imitation low roof of bright green tiles all around the edges—or so it seemed to me. The tables were dotted around the central part of the room, I am sure there was a small orchestra playing, just like in the tea room at another Lyons Corner House at the end of the Strand. Going there had up until then, been the height of my treats out. There were waiters dressed in black with white napkins laid on their left arms and one of them held out the wine in a long basket to Uncle Jack, (I was into basket making at school so I thought this was marvellous).

What did we eat? That is a good question—for once I have no idea! I was far more interested in the waiters, the wine basket, the whole ambiance of the Brasserie and of course, the green glass roof tiles. I can still see them in my mind's eye. It was to be my cherished memory of an evening out in wartime. I thought I had been transported to another world—as indeed I had, far removed from school. My first 'grown up' evening meal out. I was probably about thirteen years old.

Up until that time a treat for me, when I was home on holiday, was having tea at the Lyons Corner House in the Strand. In the 1930s and 40s tea was still a ritual in Britain. At school we had our main meal, dinner in the middle of the day—it was not called lunch. We then had tea at about five o'clock. At home it was exactly the same routine. Sometimes we had what was known as 'high tea.' This consisted of ham, meat or fish, salad followed by bread, jam and cakes. This type of meal was often eaten when families visited each other at the weekends.

I read recently a description in a tourist guide to Britain, of an English tea as, '… finely cut cucumber sandwiches followed by dainty cakes or scones and jam,' which the guide claimed was the the norm throughout Britain today. Visitors to this country might have expected such things in the 1930s, but these days I do not think so—not in the homes of the majority of British people at least. But tea for me in the 1930s was still a highlight, especially when I went to a Lyons Corner House. They were marvellous 'halls of food,' dedicated to providing a wide variety of things for ordinary people. The restaurant that I particularly remembered was on the first floor, and if we were lucky, we could get a table by the window, which looked out onto the end of the Strand and over Trafalgar Square. The waitresses were remarkable. They must have been so tired by the end of their working day. Flexitime had not been introduced and I do not know the number of hours the women had to work for Mr Lyons, but they would have been long and hard. The kitchens were at the furthest end away from the windows and the waitresses serving those tables had to walk to length of the room carrying high on their shoulders, and supported with one hand only, large trays laden with teapots, hot water and milk jugs, cups, saucers, plates—not to mention the food! It would have been interesting to know how many miles a day these women walked.

Lyons Corner Houses were very popular and we often had to queue. As we waited on the staircase, we could look down and see the small orchestra playing in the restaurant on the ground floor. I thought this was really great. I would be eagerly awaiting my tea and thinking about the treat I would have. The knicker-bocker glories were expensive, half a crown each and far too large for me anyway—I could not see over the top of the glass to scoop out the delicious flavours of fruit, and ice cream! No, I had to think of something else. It was not until after the war that I ate my first knickerbocker glory and then it took me all my time to finish it!

Old Girls' Day at Rickmansworth, (which was always the last Saturday in June) when we hoped for good weather so we could wear our pretty summer clothes, was marked by tea in the Dining Hall. And of course, holding Old Girls' Day in June meant strawberries and cream! What a contrast to the meals we had eaten there during war time and as old girls, we all looked forward to the occasion. The other highlight of that day, was none other than the traditional School Drill. Well, it was traditional whenever I returned to the school. The old girls would sit on the balcony and cast an experienced eye on the younger generation performing below them. Were the lines as straight as they were in 'our day?' How well were they doing the Wheel? But whatever we thought, the performance was always followed by great applause.

While I was away at Rickmansworth, I was fortunate to have lived in a part of the country that was not subjected to a lot of bombing. But this was certainly not the case in Worcester Park. Although the area did not suffer the kind of intense bombardment of the London Docklands, it did not escape completely either. In the winter of 1940–41, a large number of bombs had fallen in the vicinity of Mother's house.

She already had experienced air raids during the First World War, when the sirens had sounded and the family would hurry from Waterloo to take shelter near Guy's Hospital. Now during World War II, she found herself in more danger than ever before.

During the day, she worked at the railway depot at the Bricklayer's Arms on the Old Kent Road, and many of the bombs were targeted on the East End. Making the regular journey from her house in Surrey must have been a very frightening experience, especially during air raids. Understandably, in the final years of the war, it was the flying bombs that ended up causing her the greatest distress.

As I have said before, we lived near a brick field in Worcester Park. The local railway line was in a deep cutting at the end of the back garden, hidden behind rows of beautiful trees. One evening, just as Mother was about to go out on fire watch, several bombs landed in the gardens of the two houses opposite that also backed onto the railway line. Mother felt the blast, which blew open the back door and rushed through the kitchen and hallway.

The explosions did not do any massive structural damage, no roof tiles blown off or windows broken, but they caused the ceilings and walls to crack. The ceilings had to be made safe with wooden lathes nailed in squares to prevent them from falling down. Other bombs had been dropped nearby in the recreation ground—just a road away from our house. On the opposite side of the railway in Stoneleigh, the bombing had damaged my Godmother Grace's home and injured her.

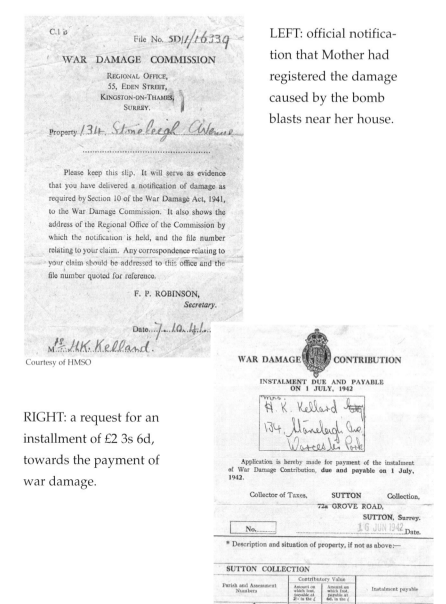

LEFT: official notification that Mother had registered the damage caused by the bomb blasts near her house.

RIGHT: a request for an installment of £2 3s 6d, towards the payment of war damage.

In my letter to Mother of May 1941, I wrote:

> I hope Auntie Grace is better and will soon be
> off the danger list.

As I noticed from the Fire Guard Report, every incident had to be recorded and handed in to the Air Raid warden. Here is an example of a report:

> Position of occurrence: 210/2 Stoneleigh
> Avenue.
> Fire: out of control.
> Remarks … no casualties.
> 1) HE near fire.
> 2) Houses all right.

HE was the abbreviation for High Explosive bomb. The second report is not so clear, but the house numbers were still quite close to our home.

> Position of occurrence: 113/15/17/19/21/23,
> Stoneleigh Avenue.
> Fire: out of control.

There are no other details on that fire guard report, but it was necessary to inform the War Damage Commission if a house had suffered any kind of damage, which also had to be paid for. Mother had made an application and was required to make contributions totalling £21 5s 0d towards the repairs carried out on Stoneleigh Avenue. She paid this through installments of £2 3s 6d on July 1 each year to the War Damage Commission. However, it was not until January 1948, after a quantity surveyor's report on the house had been completed, that the work was accepted and given to a local builder to do. I was interested to read from the

ABOVE and LEFT: my Clothing Book during the war when clothes were rationed.
BELOW and INSERT: Mother's Ration Book, issued in October 1939.

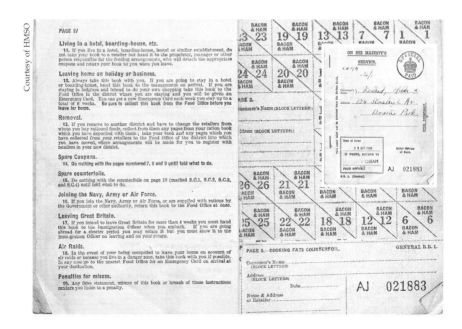

surveyor's notes that the walls needed distempering. This was a difficult task and invariably required a professional painter and decorator.

A few years later John Crabb our builder, showed Mother and me how to use emulsion paint for the first time! Imagine not knowing how to use a brush! No, we did not have a roller back then, it had yet to be invented, but I thought it was great fun helping Mother to repaint the dining room. Little did I know that I was to continue with DIY for as long as I have owned a house. And I did enjoy my first attempt at interior decorating.

By 1941 the Morrison had replaced the Anderson shelter. It was marvellous I thought, and was strong enough to withstand the weight of a two storey building falling on it. The top was made of steel and the sides were like the wire of a cage. Our new shelter was put in the dining room, in place of the table and piano, which had been moved there at the beginning of the war. There was sufficient space for a double mattress, so we could both lie down and get some sleep and rest. I still have the whistle that Mother used to hang on the wire. When I became a teacher, I would always carry it with me in my handbag every time I took children out on any educational trip from school. Old habits die hard!

And mentioning old habits, much later in life when I was married and often alone with the two children at night (my husband's job took him away from home), I used to keep by my bedside, a torch, a pair of trousers, a jumper and flat slip–on shoes. I also tied a heavy rope around the end of the radiator nearest to the window, all just in case! I must also mention it was all put away in my wardrobe before my husband arrived back home. And I still scrape the last vestiges of butter from the butter paper, still push the jam or marmalade down the sides of the jar so that it does not stay on the side and dry up! And there are many more little saving tips which people do of course, that have been handed down, but I was not at home to learn a lot of them.

What could my Grandmother have taught me? She knew all the cuts of meat and how to cook them. Brought up at school, I had not come near a joint of meat of any kind and just passed two ration books to the butcher and received in exchange a rolled up piece of beef with fat tied on the outside.

Rationing had been introduced in 1940, the first time since 1918. Our meat ration in March 1940 was one shilling and ten pence worth and later between one and two shillings. Ration coupons were not required for offal, rabbit, poultry, game, fish, sausages and meat pies. By 1941, prices were frozen on certain types of food like coffee, cocoa, rice and spaghetti. I am surprised there were any of the above foods considering the areas in the world they were imported from. It was not just the food that was rationed. Coal and coke were too. Supplies of coal, which had once been sent by sea to large cities like London, were now dispatched on the congested railways. And the carriages were left unheated and dim—the compartment lights an erie shade of blue. Unlike today, the homes of the majority of people during the 1940s were not built with central heating. Houses before the war

Food Rationing (serving per person, per week)		Imperial System oz = ounce s = shilling d = penny	Metric and Decimal 1 oz = 28.35 grams 1 shilling = 5 pence 1 d = 1 pence
		Initial Ration	Later Variations
January 1940	Bacon or ham	4 oz	4–8 oz
	Butter	4 oz	2–4 oz
	Sugar	12 oz	8–12 oz
March 1940	Meat	1 s 10 d worth	1–2 s
July 1940	Tea	2 oz	2–4 oz
March 1941	Preserves	2 oz	2–4 oz
May 1941	Cheese	1 oz	1–8 oz
	Margarine & fats	6 oz	6 oz
Nov 1941	Tinned foods	4 points	4–5 points
July 1942	Sweets	2 oz	2–3 oz

Source: Ministry of Food

had fireplaces in every room and that included the bedrooms. I was used to living in one room, where the fire was lit and that was all the heating in the house and often it was not even lit until the evening.

So how did we start the fire? We did not have any logs. And it certainly was not the custom in this country as it is in France for example, where they specialise in wood burning stoves, to have outside stores full of wood. We relied on coal, coke and anthracite as fuels to heat our houses and water. Certain vegetables and fruit—tomatoes for example, came in boxes or punnets made from very thin strips of wood, the thickness of bark. They would have been used to help light the fire. Sometimes it was not always possible to obtain even these.

So the problem was solved by using the daily newspaper. But it was not just scrumpled up—although some pages would have been used like this. As we did not have a television or video, only the radio to listen to, a useful task for the evening was to take a sheet of paper, start at one corner with a slightly wet finger and begin to turn over the edge so that it began to roll smoothly. The secret was to try to get the paper as tight as possible, then we twisted it and folded in the edges. These little bundles were a tremendous help in getting a fire started because the paper burnt slowly, allowing the small pieces of wood or warm embers to catch light. Whenever we cleaned out the grate, we took care to keep the embers if possible.

Sometimes of course, the fire had burned completely to ash, but quite often there were several pieces of coal that had not burned totally away. In order to save our precious coal allowance, Mother had special fire bricks installed on either side of the grate. This made a smaller fire admittedly, but was also more economical. And coal fires had one big advantage—we could make mouth watering toast. Delia Smith was absolutely right when she said in one of her television programmes that there is nothing so good as toast made in front of an open fire. For this you require a toasting fork. These were readily available and often very decorative. The prongs were pushed into the bread and then it was held in front of the fire. Even today, it still beats the electric pop up toaster every time!

In Mother's house, water for washing and bathing was heated by a little free standing boiler in the kitchen. This boiler used coke as a fuel and was only lit at the weekends. If we needed hot water for washing, a kettle was boiled and taken to the bathroom, where there was never any heating!

Did we smell? Yes, I am sure we must have, but then so did everyone else! There were advertisements that encouraged people to use 'Life Buoy' soap for washing under their arms! This was a cheaper alternative to deodorants, which were not readily available. The one I remember best was 'Mum,' but it was extra money. Soap and hot water properly and regularly used cost a lot less! The cleaning of clothes, as I have mentioned before, presented the women with problems. Detergents as we know them today did not exist, it was soap powder and the washboard in the sink with a bar of 'Sunlight Soap' and a lot of physical hand rubbing that got clothes clean.

Mother was always most particular in regularly brushing all her outer garments before and after wearing them. Thanks to her, I now have a good collection of large very strong bristle brushes. She could not afford to send clothes to the cleaners and during the war I do not know whether this service existed or not. Besides, I was away from all these problems, I only encountered them for a few weeks a year when I returned home from school for the holidays. I was cushioned from the everyday chores and the worries of running a home.

Although we did have our little cleaning duties to perform each day at school. Pat and I had one of the Prefect's studies as our morning duty, but that was as far as general housework went. In the bathroom, we had to keep our linen towels neatly folded on the rail under our wash basin. The linen brush and comb bags, each with our House number, had to be all neatly arranged in a line and hung along one wall. And as for the counterpane on our beds, well there was no need for any inspection, because we all took such pride in the appearance of our beds and so of course, the look of the whole dormitory.

I was in the third year before we were asked to help with the clearing away and washing up of the crockery and cutlery. Well, what fun we had! As I have said, there were so many of us in Zetland House that we frequently made any task we were given into a great game. It was the first time any of us had set foot in the kitchens and we knew next to nothing about who worked there or how our food was prepared.

I thought that aiming the large plates accurately between the huge rotating bristle brushes in the vast stainless steel sinks, was great fun. We developed a real skill at doing this with the dirty plates. Then another girl retrieved them, dipped them in a sink for rinsing and finally into racks to dry.

This was also the first time I had seen the slicing machines that cut up the very long loaves of bread. Were they specially baked for us, or was the bread baked at school? I do not know, however the machines were very impressive. None of this was a chore, because we had made it fun, but then of course we spoilt things, like nearly all young people do when they get carried away with an idea and become silly.

There were large three tiered trolleys in the kitchen and we discovered that we could sit between the middle and bottom shelves and with a bit of initial pushing, propel ourselves forward using our hands. After a little practice, we were soon whizzing up and down the beautiful dining room, between the rows of tables! I thought this was great. And of course we did not stop to think for one minute that we might cause any damage. So it is with children, once they get caught up in some silly prank they never think about the consequences of their actions.

When I look back and reflect on the incident now, I am appalled we could have been so stupid! Then most things seem different at the time. I am sure that whoever was in charge of us in the kitchens, soon put a stop to our little games. We probably lost marks for the House (Zetland never did win the Conduct Cup whilst I was there!) and shortly afterwards our spell of duty in the kitchen came to an abrupt end.

We did learn to look after our clothes though. Every Saturday morning, once lessons had finished, we went back to our own House. The Prefects and Sub–Prefects sat two to each Common Room with their decade. As I mentioned, there were four dormitories to a House, four Prefects and two Sub–Prefects. The Senior House Prefect was in Dormitory One and so on down the line of seniority.

As there were fifty girls to a House we were divided between the four Prefects—into a decade, which was made up of girls from every year group. (I know the maths is not quite right, because in some decades there were eleven girls). On Saturday mornings, we all sat together with a Prefect around a long trestle table. Our underclothes, pyjamas, white collars, all numbered in Indian ink, were handed out. It was our responsibility to mend our own clothes, have them inspected and passed by the Prefect or House Matron. Once they were handed in, we were free to go. I need hardly tell you that I was always one of the first to finish by midday, so I could enjoy my free time!

Our lives at school were very strictly regulated by bells, just as they had been at Weybridge; the getting up bell, the saying prayers bell (we had to be bathed, washed and dressed by this time) usually about a quarter past seven in the morning. By the next bell, we were ready to assemble in the Senior Common Room, our beds made and hair brushed. We lined up in decades, two one side of the centre door, two opposite.

Miss Vickridge (Vic) wearing spectacles, stood sternly in the doorway with her arms crossed, hair plaited and turned into a bun. The Prefects inspected their decade and if we had lost any marks the previous day, we had to inform them. The Prefects then reported to Vic, telling her the name of the girl and the number of marks lost, which would eventually appear on the girl's term report under 'conduct.'

I can understand this really. There were four hundred of us in the senior school. We all had quite a lot of belongings to account for, in addition to all our clothes, which had to be in the cupboards at the end of the dormitories. Some outer coats were left in the cloakrooms on the ground floor. There was a space for keeping our shoes too. We each had a locker in which to keep personal belongings and our Hymn and Prayer Books, Psalter and Bible. Everything was numbered with the House initial and the number that we had been given on entering the House.

We were liable to loose a mark for anything that was left lying about—it was easy to know to whom it belonged—no use saying, "Oh, it's not mine," there was no escape! All these lost marks were added up at the end of the school year and the Conduct Cup awarded to the House with the least number of marks. But you could loose a conduct mark for grave misdemeanors, which counted for twenty ordinary marks and you had to report after morning assembly in the main hall to the Headmistress, Miss Fryer, in front of the entire school. We all knew why a girl was walking up the steps onto the stage and so we made sure never to be called up.

The School Drill, performed every Tuesday at midday, was both a ritual and a tradition. Like it or not, I think that we would all confess to being secretly proud of taking part in it. We wore white blouses and Masonic blue gymslips. These were not the usual variety conjured up by the mention of gymslips—a box pleat from a small square neck yoke to the hem and tied with a girdle. Oh, no! These were stylish with a fitted bodice, square neck line and slightly flared 'A' line skirt. The combination of blue and white was very smart and the effect as we went through our routines striking.

We were ordered into sizes, (little had changed from Weybridge!) in twos, yet again. Age had nothing to do with it, so Tris who was tall and in the third year (now Year 9) might find that her partner was in the Sixth From (Year 13) and conversely a shorter seventeen year old could find that her partner was a junior!

By kind permission of the Royal Masonic School for Girls

Performing the Wheel, during the School Drill.

By kind permission of the Royal Masonic School for Girls

This is the end of the Drill, performed before George VI and Queen Elizabeth, when we made the Masonic emblems of the Compass and Square.

We lined up with our partners in the classroom corridor, this extended from Cumberland to Ruspini House. From here we went into the hall, to the accompaniment of music, with the music teachers playing the grand pianos. One of the PE staff stood on the right hand side of the stage and she gave us our instructions. Every movement was performed to music and we had to remain in line and in perfect time with everyone else. The effect from the balcony was very dramatic, with the white arms of the blouses making a distinct pattern.

We were in rows going from the front (smaller) to the back (tallest) of the hall. I think it was probably eight rows across. Sometimes alternate rows stood, whilst others knelt on the floor. The pattern was made by the rows moving their arms in different directions—but whatever the movement, everyone had to have their arms at exactly the same angle as the girl in front and also the same as the other rows across the hall, precision was all important.

We did marching and counter marching, but the highlight of the performance was the wheel. The routines were very cleverly thought out. We arrived at the right place, at the right time to the music, ready to perform the next set of movements. So it was with the wheel. Somehow in the pattern of marching, we made spokes, the shortest girls in the centre radiating out to the tallest girls at the end of the 'spoke' line.

Then on a command from the mistress and a chord struck on the piano, the last three girls in the spoke would peel off to the right or left and follow each other in a circle around the outside, whilst the spokes of the wheel with heads turned, again to the left or right depending on which direction that particular wheel was turning, would march in a circle. We knew where we should be by listening to the music that was being played. When the third tallest girl reached her 'spoke' for the second time, she joined the line followed by the last two girls. The accomplishment of this routine whenever it was performed on Prize Day, or Old Girls' Day, was always received with great applause. The final counter marching led into the Masonic symbols of the Compass and Square.

I remember very clearly making the white blouses that we wore for the occasion. I thought I was managing to sew splendidly, not letting Jackie get too far ahead of me. Then to my consternation when I went to Miss Atherton (who was the needlework teacher and Head of Ruspini House), she told me to unpick all the French seams because I had made them much too wide. To my surprise Jackie finished her blouse, well ahead of me and I never made half inch French seams ever again. I did not like being left behind!

Every evening after tea we had 'prep'—not called homework of course. The time varied, as it still does today in all schools. Prep started I think between half past six and a quarter to seven in the evening, this was held in the two Common Rooms. The Prefects worked in their studies. We were all allocated a place at one of the trestle tables. The juniors always went up to bed at an earlier time than the rest of the House. We had a glass of milk and then sometimes a biscuit or a bun or oat cakes, which I remember I did not like because they were so dry, not realising of course how nutritious they were. A member of our House staff would be on duty and generally oversee the evening. But we were not involved in prep at the weekends—until of course we reached the years when we had to prepare for the important external Cambridge exams.

Then we had to keep working during most of our free time. Yes, we had quite a lot of free time and it had to be filled. When we were in the Junior Common Room we devised many ways of keeping busy. With so many of us the same age, it was easier to devise games in which we could all take part and of course there were always enough of us to make up the numbers. For example, after 'Monopoly' or card games such as 'Solo' someone might suggest, "Why don't we play… sardines … or go to the Dell?"

We used to go to 'The Dell' a lot and I liked it. I thought the trees were beautiful and there was a huge dip in the middle. This meant that we could run up and down the sides, and hide behind the trees.

Cowboys and Indians was a favourite game, which I mention in a letter to Mother:

> Last Sunday evening we were playing down in the Dell and someone threw a stone and it hit one of our girls on the forehead, first of all she did not cry but the bump came up awfully quickly. We all flew down from our posts and

crowded round her. When we said, "June doesn't it hurt?" then she started to cry. Poor thing it must have hurt, but now it has quite gone, but her head has turned a little green in colour!

I am surprised that we did not have many more accidents, perhaps we did and I just did not record them. Near the Dell was a line of lovely old Spanish chestnut trees. They were behind the netball and tennis courts. One of our games was to find a big stick and throw it up at the branches. We did this only in the autumn when the trees were full of chestnuts, and not enough of them had fallen on the ground for our liking!

I know that today I would be appalled at the thought of damaging the trees by such behaviour, but then we were concentrating on the chestnuts and how many we could eat and get away with before we got caught. It was easy to break open the case—we just stamped on it and out popped the nut. Sometimes of course the chestnut was not fully ripe but this did not deter us. They were not brown with leathery skins like the ones bought in shops. These were still pale and it was easy to bite the top off and peel away the pithy skin. This was not nice, leaving an unpleasant taste in our mouths but then we were left with the sweet soft chestnut to eat. I have never really liked the cooked chestnuts we can buy today, I much prefer the unripe ones!

I recall spending cold winter afternoons probably a Saturday, with my knees against one of the radiators in the Common Room munching chestnuts. The radiators were not on in the dormitories and I complained to Mother in one letter written early during the war. I do not know why, because we did not have any heating in our own home!

We enjoyed inventing and playing all kinds of games, usually involving some kind of chasing and inevitably we were noisy. I can still remember the time when we devised a game with trestle tables. The idea was for two girls to race each other the length of the Common Room from the door (very important this!) to the windows at the other end. Each girl sat on the middle of a table. By moving our feet and bottoms actively enough we could make the tables move. We took it in turns and then probably made up two teams to race against each other. The sound we made must have been truly ear splitting, for not only were the tables noisy, so were we. Everyone was shouting, cheering on their team representative. Then my turn came. I was in my element. Shrieking and waving my arms, I managed to propel the table to the end of the room. I do not recall who my opponent was, neither was I aware that the rest of my team had suddenly become very quiet. But eventually it dawned on me that I was actually the only one left in the Common Room who was making any noise. As I came to a standstill, I became aware of the other girls' frozen faces and the descent of complete silence and stillness—nobody moved. Still sitting on the table, I turned around and saw Vic standing under the clock in front of the double swing doors, her arms folded and a very stern expression on her face.

I do not recall the actual reprimand, but for the punishment I was sent up to Dormitory Two and told to sit on the pipes between the rows of beds. My opponent was sent to Dormitory Three—also to sit on pipes. This could have been Tris, because she remembers the incident too. There was to be no talking whatsoever between us. All right, we were too far away to talk or whisper, but I could still see Tris, as the double doors to the dormitories had been left open.

After a while, probably not a very long time, we became bored. I do not know who started the next game, but off came our shoes and we both tried to slide them over to each other. This was easy, because all the floors at school except the cloakrooms and bathrooms, were parquet and beautifully polished. This episode probably ended with a bell telling us it was time to go to the dining room for tea.

I think we must have found that the hours of Saturday afternoon and evening hung heavily, with not a great deal to do. So we used our imagination to make up plays and dances. Then one Saturday evening, someone suggested that if we blacked our faces, we could put on a minstrel show, which would involve singing and dancing. I was probably instrumental in this suggestion as I liked these kinds of activity.

Here is an extract from Mother's diary, April 7, 1934:

> Auntie Maisie and Uncle Leonard gave a concert. You were Mickey Mouse and a great success you made. It was your first appearance on the concert stage. You are fond of dancing and singing and I often wonder what you will do when you enter the business world in years ahead!

The only black substance we could lay our hands on was shoe polish. We would have found this in the cloakroom areas on the ground floor. With blackened faces, we made up songs, and performed our little singing and dancing routines. But now the real dilemma presented itself. How could we get ourselves clean?

All the floors at school were made of beautifully polished wood, as were the stair cases and banisters leading to the dormitories. So up the junior staircase we crept to reach the bathroom of Dormitory Three.

Remember we wore white collars on our dresses. We had white linen towels. The white and red lined brush and comb bags were all hanging in a neat line. The whole place would have been shining and spotlessly clean, just like every other part of the school. No wonder Miss Smith, our House Matron was distraught at what she saw that Saturday evening. No wonder we were commanded to stand still. No wonder she could not deal with us but had to fetch Miss Vickridge. What a sight they must have seen. Little eleven and twelve year old girls trying to wash black shoe polish off their faces and failing miserably in preventing it from getting all over their white collars, white towels, white wash basins, tiles and comb bags, door handles—everywhere in fact.

We got a very severe telling off from Vic. We had to scrub and wash everything. It took us a very long time, taking up the whole of Saturday evening and needless to say, we never tried it again.

Mentioning the staircase reminds me of another incident. At the very top of the houses were the maids' bedrooms, though we never saw them, for being wartime they would have been called up into one of the services or the land army. Or maybe the people who cleaned the school did not sleep there, but only came during the day.

Anyway, Jackie had decided to find out what it was like on the top floor. I can remember her leading us up the stairs (we were strictly forbidden to go back to the dormitories during the day), nor were we ever allowed up the second staircase. This was all no man's land to us. Who were we going to meet? Fortunately, on this occasion nobody. We entered the little bedrooms in the roof and Jackie found a gramophone. In the letter of June 14, 1942, after I have described the symphony concert, I wrote:

> There is not much news except that we have found an old gramophone up in the top of the House with some records. The records and the gramophone are all right, it's only the needles and they are awful.

Then there is a scrappy piece of paper with a PS:

> Please Mummy do you think you could bring a few needles and records for our gramophone? Records like 'Post Horn Gallop,' and some nice waltzes PLEASE. We all want some, because we

have no music in the Common Room and it is
very dull so PLEASE Mummy.
All my love,
Babs.

I think the little PS says it all. Life was dull and Vic had a sense
of humour, though at the time we did not appreciate it and she
must have realised that it was just mischief we were getting into
because we were bored. We were not rude or impertinent or
insolent. There was no malice in all the 'pranks' we devised. We
were only little girls trying to fill in the days, all of the same age
with not a lot to interest us.

But this was not the case all the time. I said we enjoyed doing
plays and had come up with an idea for a screen—we must have

The 'Just William' programme for our little production.

asked Matron for an old sheet. We strung this across the Common Room, probably two girls holding either side, shone our torches on it and made shadow plays. These were a great success and I remember inviting a few girls from the Senior Common Room to come and watch them. Dawn was also good at English and we had started to read the 'Just William' books. Dawn rewrote the stories into little plays and we were all given a part. No need to ask who got to be William—Jackie of course. For some reason I have never been able to fathom, I was chosen to act the part of Mrs Brown. These plays occupied a lot our time in many ways. I even found a copy of a programme.

In February 1941, I wrote to Mother:

> On Wednesday next, Margaret, you know the one I pointed out to you down the village, well she and some other girls are giving a fancy dress party. The other night we had to pick bits of paper with people from nursery rhymes. I picked Cindarella, so I have to dress up as her.
>
> After I have finished writing to you, I am going out in the garden to play sardines with some of the girls. I do hope you get a job and are kept safe. Well, I think this is all for now so goodbye till next Sunday.
>
> All my love and kisses from your loving little daughter,
> Barbara.

We also liked going to 'The Pond' as we called it, which was down the cinder path. This was located just behind Ruspini and Zetland Houses. The pond was at the bottom of the hill and near the walled kitchen gardens. These were strictly out of bounds and

I do not ever remember venturing inside. We liked to watch the tadpoles swimming, but I was not so keen about all the little frogs they turned into, hopping all over the place.

There was a very large walnut tree on one side of the pond. Pat and I would often be there in the autumn trying to find walnuts. To our annoyance most of the walnuts fell into the water as the main part of the tree overhung the pond. Sometimes during winter, it froze and of course we tried to slide on it, but we always got found out by the Prefects. It was probably part of their duty to patrol in that area.

The school grounds were very large and being wartime, we were restricted as to where we could go. This was perfectly understandable because of the sudden air raids that we were likely to have. But that did not prevent us from making the most of the areas where we were allowed. Treasure hunts were a great favourite. In February 1942, I wrote to Mother, obviously very pleased with myself:

> On Wednesday we had a treasure hunt all over the grounds, finding a clue which tells you something about the next clue. Granny (Pat) and I won the pieces of paper, which was the prize. Granny and I came first in finding it.

Not much by the standards of today, but it did not matter to us, we had never been used to receiving special prizes and just to take part and then win the game was enough.

Mentioning special prizes, I had managed to win one in 1940, my last year as a little girl in Weybridge. (We were of course living at Rickmansworth by then). It was a certificate for drawing and painting. I remember being so disappointed, as I had looked forward to something special—not a piece of paper, however nicely it was presented with the school badge and an aerial view of the school buildings—but as it says on the certificate: 'The money which would have been expended in purchasing it (a prize) should instead be sent to the Red Cross and Order of St John War Fund.' We all had to make some sacrifices to help others and receiving a piece of paper was appropriate when children of my age were in such danger through out the rest of Europe.

The trenches were in an area, needless to say, that was out of bounds, even though they were so close to Zetland House. We were not allowed to go near them, except of course when ordered to and taken there by a member of staff in an air raid.

At the time, there were two large mounds one either end of the trenches. The one that Zetland used was straight opposite the House, across the grass, passed the sandbags into the 'hole,' and down the steps. The entrance to the other trench was behind another mound of earth in a kind of semi–circle. This hid the entrance. We had become bored again, so we decided to go into the garden. Soon we found ourselves playing 'It' out of sight, around the end trench. But it was not long before someone suggested that a game of 'murder' or 'sardines,' would be even more fun.

The trench was pitch black inside, the main passage twisted and turned. Negotiating our way through was not so easy. Then there were sudden cul–de–sacs at the sides. Trying to find who was hiding where, turned out to be quite impossible. Not surprisingly therefore, we ended up playing just inside the trench entrance. But of course, our blue Masonic dresses offered no camouflage against the green of nature and for some reason, Prefects always seemed to go around in pairs. So predictably enough, two from Ruspini House appeared at the wrong moment and accused us of playing out of bounds.

"No," we protested, "we were not actually in the trench, we were only playing around it."

But despite our version of events, they did not believe us. Poor Vic, all her girls were always in trouble. What would she do with us? It was July and just before Sports Day. We had quite a promising team that year in 1942. Joyce was a good runner so was June, who excelled at long distances and we had great hopes that the junior section of the House would do well.

Vic decided that our punishment would be to stay in the trench on Sports Day. And as luck would have it, it turned out to be the hottest day of the month. So that was how we ended up spending our time—sitting in the heat, with nothing to occupy ourselves. We sat on the hard benches immediately inside the entrance. We were not allowed to bring anything with us. Vic though had her knitting to keep her occupied. After some considerable time sitting motionless in complete silence, except for the repetitive click click of Vic's knitting needles, one of us began to find this amusing and I do not need to tell you what a group of thirteen year old girls is like when they start to giggle. But Vic understood us much better than I personally gave her credit for. "All right," she said at last, "you may go and join the sports."

How we all ran down to the sports field! There was no need to point out the girls who were in the junior house relay team. They arrived at the start line so quickly, they were in time to take part in the race and yes, they won! I have always thought of that as a thank you token to Vic and a sort of reward to her, at least we won something for the House and an acknowledgement that the punishment she had devised fitted the crime.

We did not always have to find something to occupy ourselves and pass the time. At various stages in our school life we rehearsed for Committee Days. On 21 July, 1940, I wrote to Mother:

> On Thursday it was Committee Day and some
> girls in our form did a play. I was in it and I was
> the KING.
> On Saturday the Prefects had a party.

These were probably the senior girls who were leaving. There was often a vaulting exhibition and I assumed all the girls involved had been specially picked, as their performances were always very good. My form also did poetry readings, short gym displays and piano recitals. All these events needed practising because they just had to be perfect for the Committee; everything had to run like 'clockwork.' The senior girls were often doing plays (not necessarily on Committee Day) and I looked forward to these very much. We also had lantern lectures.

Sometimes musicians came to the school. On one occasion we had a visit from a Belgian group. There were always concerts to rehearse for and then there were the dances.

> May 25, 1941.
> On Thursday it was Committee Day, and in the evening our form did a gym display in the hall. Another form, I think it was selected girls from the Fifth and Sixth Forms, did vaulting over the horse and the box. It was lovely. After that we had dances, 'The Chestnut Tree' and a waltz. In 'The Chestnut Tree' one of the ladies asked Dawn, Eileen and myself if she could come with us. So we said yes. We had to teach her the dance as she did not know it. She did not have an English accent, but I could not tell where she came from.

Miss Atherton taught us to dance. I already had a head start, because Mother had been teaching me at home from an early age and had entered me into a dancing competition, held on the stage at the Odeon Cinema in Worcester Park, in the 1930s. I remember not liking the very bright light shining on my face, and kept looking out to the wings to see Mother—this was of course the era of Shirley Temple! As we were obviously all girls, we had to learn to lead in the dances as well as follow. I am sure those of us who were at the school during my time, will recall the large circle we danced in—not near any of the staff—who had to remain seated around the outside of the hall, during this performance rather like wallflowers!

We also had dances in the House. This happened when we were in the Senior Common Room. Vic used to play the piano and had taught us mainly the 'country dances' as they were called, such as the 'Sir Roger de Coverly.' I liked that one and we happily all joined in. 'The Dashing White Sergeant,' was another favourite of mine. By the time I left school I had quite a repertoire.

Everyone enjoyed the next incident even though it ended with a punishment! Snow had fallen and remained on the ground. Either we were allowed out to play or we had taken it upon ourselves to go out anyway. Whatever the reason, we decided to play snowballs. What else?

There was a tarmacadam area between the houses and it was here that we scooped up the snow and started to have a good game, throwing snowballs at each other. This was fine and we were having such fun until suddenly a snowball missed its intended target and whizzed into the Common Room through a window that had been accidentally left open. Then someone threw another one after it and soon we all joined in, snowballs cascading into the Common Room. Eventually Vic arrived on the scene and was very cross, as you can imagine. We had to clear

Caught on camera! The guilty participants of the snowball fight!

away all the snow, which by then had heavily coated the floor. Going down on our hands and knees, we had to scrub everywhere. If you ask Tris today, she would be able to give you a very good rendition of, "Oh to be, oh to be a char, working all the day, so tra, la, la, la, la." We sang as we scrubbed. Again, the punishment fitted the crime. But the first snowball really had been thrown through the open window accidentally.

We were not always up to mischief! We had decided that after the success of the first bazaar, we should raise money for our men on the merchant navy ship, and try our hardest to do another one. By the Autumn and Spring terms of 1943 and 1944, we were very busy indeed making more items to sell—remember, this was an internal event and we only had the members of staff and the other girls as potential customers.

Our mothers were involved again and of course they all gave us their utmost support. Tris's mother painted a lovely little oil painting, I remember it being like a traditional English cottage garden. I am writing to Mother in 1943:

> The girls have brought back some lovely things for the bazaar. The toy stall has got twenty five things. I have reserved you one picture. It is quite a big one and will probably cost six shillings and nine pence, so you will have to hope that it's not too dear, of course that's only what we say it will be, but Tris the girl whose mother painted it, says it should go for ten shillings, but we don't take any notice of what she says! (Tris has been one of my closest friends all my life—so much for being a teenager).
>
> Would you believe it, I have lost weight again. I now weigh 6st 13lbs 4oz and last term I was seven stone something (remembering numbers

was not a strong point of mine!) I shall have to do something about it won't I? Today, we had some lovely chocolate but it cost us three pence, still we don't mind as it was milk with toffee inside—it's lovely. I am Form Prefect again this term, ho–hum!

We can do it (the bazaar). Miss Fryer said last term she would say yes this term, so we have picked four more girls to go to her, so we wish them luck. I am in School Drill this year and in the third row from the front worse luck, but we are jolly glad we are not in the singing—the other fourth form is though, (we must have been rehearsing for something special).

We have got £1.0.0 already. Two girls wanted something for another girl's birthday so we sold them a lovely powder puff in a georgette hanky and that green necklace of yours for ten shillings, together with my five shillings, Granny's three and six and chuck penny two shillings. Please! Please! Please! will you make a dolly and only if you have time would you be a darling and make another one! (thank you). Evidently they (the other girls with the toy stall) want the dolly to have three bits of hair sticking out of her head with ribbon tied on the ends.

Well, I must close now.
Your loving little daughter,
Barbara.

In another letter I am writing:

> Please make lots more things if you can, because
> all the other mothers are making things. One
> girl's mother is making pictures, so please try
> and make lots more. You know that black velvet
> that we have got at home, you could make it
> into shoe polishers if you want to and we would
> like some kettle holders if you could possibly
> make some. Please will you send me some
> material as much as you can spare. Floral or
> ordinary and the pattern, as we want to make
> animals and please ask anybody you can think
> of if they will please turn out anything they can
> spare. You know the kind of things we had last
> time, we have quite a bit but not nearly enough.
>
> We have had a good many air raids at the
> beginning of the term. The siren went the other
> night but we did not have to get up. If you have
> time, do you think that you could go to the
> funny little shop and see if you can find any
> more funny little things.
>
> This is all for now.
> Lots of Love, from your loving little daughter,
> Barbara

Goodness knows where or what 'the funny little shop' was
that I refer to or what the 'funny little things' were they sold.
Although, I was sorry to hear that Mother had gone to bed very
early one evening, (she had a bad cold) I wrote:

> Glad that you felt better last week so that you were able to do the bazaar stuff. But all the same, I am sorry to hear that your cold has not completely gone.

Poor Mother, always being pestered by me for something and now with this second bazaar under way, we were working very hard. I think we spent most of our spare time making things. There was one advantage for Mother being employed as a Welfare Officer on the Southern Railways and doing office work. It allowed her to sew in the evenings! And sew she certainly did.

> Yes, the girls did like the things which you made. Granny's mother came yesterday. She brought some lovely things, two lovely beds, a lovely big knitted mouse and giraffe and four more little dolls. The toy stall has got about forty four things. They are getting on aren't they?

It seems incredible now, reading these extracts from my letters about the bazaar, that I can only recall very little of what we actually produced. I know there were various felt 'creatures' and a cute little Humpty Dumpty figure made from coloured strips of material. I remember these in particular, as some of them became my mascots, which I placed in front of me on my desk when I sat the School Certificate exams.

Mother's effort was tremendous and the standard of finish so professional. I liked the white velvet bull dog best. She had made an animal so appropriate for that time in the country's history and synonymous with Winston Churchill of course. It was a really well made toy and we wanted to charge quite a lot for it, but we were not allowed to, so someone ended up with a bargain! One of my main memories from the period, was the excitement created at the end of dinner time when our House Matron, Mrs Darnel, emerged from the kitchen area carrying parcels. She was smiling and giving a nod to each girl who was anticipating a parcel from their mothers. Then there was the dash to the House after we had been dismissed. No, of course we were not allowed to run along the corridors—but we did not pay any attention. Our focus was on getting back to the House and then to the linen room as quickly as possible, where we would crowd around the opening of the parcels with great excitement to see what new items for the bazaar had been sent.

I did not know of the existence of the following letter from Miss Vickridge to Mother until I found it amongst a little pile of letters all tied together. It says everything:

> Dear Mrs Kelland,
>
> Today being the day after our Bazaar, I felt I must write a little note thanking you for all you have done to further its success. The children are exalted: they raised £28 odd. I think it is an excellent result, especially at this end of a 'Wings for Victory' week here! What I liked most was the way in which the children ran it from the first to the last, showing a development from last time.
>
> They made lots of toys, inspired by the lovely ones you made.A grown ups ingenuity and handiwork set a standard for children to aim at, and the things you so kindly sent not only graced the stalls, but also gave them examples of what to make, how to make it, and how to finish it off. The big velvet toy is lamented by several members of the Staff: the Headmistress bore it off in triumph! It was lovely. I shall

treasure my kettle holder as a pleasant memory
of a very successful day: thank you very much!

Yours sincerely,
Margaret E. M. Vickridge.

By now things had changed at home. Grandmother had died
in 1943. I remember the sad visiting day in June of that year when
Mother told me the news. Since my birth, Grandmother had been
with me constantly. Mother never had to worry while she went
out to work. I was safe at home. There were no pre-school
nurseries in those days or childminders. Grandmother's death
was a great loss to me. It would also mean that now I would be
left alone during the school holidays.

Fortunately, we had friends who had moved to Worcester Park
at the same time as us. The women were also on their own during
the day, and were often very happy for me to keep them company.
I remember spending hours with Mrs Sainty whilst she knitted.
Her daughter, Peggy was several years older than me and she
would have gone out to work. Then when the local schools broke
up for the holidays, there were always May, Kenneth and Alan.
We made a foursome and would spend the days together. It was
not a 'girlfriend boyfriend situation,' we were just friends.

We were often warned about the dangers of German airmen,
who after parachuting from their planes, might try to hide in a
back garden or a house. We were told to be constantly on our
guard. During one of her many trips to Ireland, a friend had given
Mother a Shilleleigh. This was a short piece of branch from the
blackthorn tree, with a decorative cord in a loop at the smooth
end. Mother took it off the wall by the fireplace and left it just
inside the front door so that she could easily find it when she
entered her dark home in the evening. She then went into every
room swinging her Shilleleigh and was quite happy doing this
until the day she read in a national newspaper, about an Irish

woman whose nickname was Shilleleigh Kate. Poor Kate had been hit on the head with her own Shilleleigh—and died! That as you can imagine put paid to Mother's home security routine. She had to be very brave and go into her house hoping everything would be all right.

By the September of 1943, we became increasingly aware of a lot more activity from our own aircraft. I wrote to Mother:

> We have had some more gliders over this week.
> Yesterday, we saw many planes coming back,
> some were quite damaged.

Now that Grandmother had died, Mother had to do everything in the house and garden by herself. When we had been all living together, Grandmother had looked after the home and did the cooking. Mother and I ate our meals with my Grandparents in their dining–living room. Grandfather had tended the garden and grown the vegetables. Mother was the one who went out to work and earnt money for the family, teaching at Bloomsbury and working on the treadle machine on her various corset assignments.

In the winter time of 1943-44, it cannot have been pleasant going into that cold house on her own. There would have been no cheery fire to warm her, no kettle ready on the gas stove for her first cup of tea. She might have had a difficult journey from Nine Elms. Trains were often diverted, they were cold and dimly lit and the journey may have taken longer than normal. But she had to keep on going and persevere. At least she was reasonably safe, sleeping on her own in the Morrison shelter, rather than the damp and dark Anderson shelter that had been in the garden.

And of course I was growing up all the time. It became my responsibility when home on holiday, to go to the shops in Worcester Park and get the food. Perhaps this is why I remember the queues so well. Mother started to buy in London and what vegetables she was able to carry, for she had at least a twenty minute walk uphill from the station to her home. It must have seemed a little strange—she was once again buying from the shops in the Cut and the Marsh, just as she had done when she first lived at Waterloo on arriving from the west of Ireland at the age of twelve.

In September 1943, we were still having air raids during the day. I remember one particularly well that occurred in the summer term. Marie had come back from the holidays with her hair done in what was then called an 'Eton Crop.'

Naturally, we all wanted a style like that because it was marvellous for when we went swimming; we could quickly and easily dry our hair. And we were always going to the swimming pool, asking Miss Elliot if we could help out. We knew that if she said, "Yes," then there was a chance we would be allowed to have 'extra' time in the pool. In my early letters from Rickmansworth, I always told Mother about my latest efforts, whether I managed to swim the width of the bath at the deep end, scull or jump off the third diving board or learn to dive correctly.

And I was always trying to find something exciting to write about too. So this turned out to be the day when I was having my hair cut by a visiting hairdresser and the sirens had gone off. We both hurried outside, heading in the direction of the trenches.

But only one side of my hair had been finished—the other side was still the same long length. Just like the dressing gown episode, I was pointed at and comments were made. Ridicule is very hard to bear whatever your age and the ridicule from the other girls has helped imprint this episode on my mind.

I had also started to read more, for I had discovered John Buchan's books. I would spend an hour or so with 'The Thirty Nine Steps' and 'Green Mantle,' and then after lights out in the dormitory, I retold the stories. It was very easy for one person to stop talking as soon as we heard the footsteps of the duty teacher approaching, so that by the time she looked in, everything was peaceful and quiet. No shushing or giggling and rustling of sheets, all the give aways of children not settling down to sleep. I think perhaps we may have had enough punishments already. But if we ever did get caught talking, the usual command was, "Get out of bed! Put on your dressing gown and slippers and go down to the Common Room!"

Once there we had to fetch our Psalters (our book of psalms) from our lockers, we were given paper and invariably had to start writing out Psalm 108. I seem to recall that this was the longest of them all. How much time we spent in the Common Room I do not remember, but we were very soon ready to return to the dormitory, settle down and go to sleep.

Perhaps I was going to heed Mother's comments, which she made in the only letter that I now have from her:

> So you are doing a lot of reading. Sorry to hear that it was not school books for the exams. My dear, you will never get a chance again to learn and I do want you to have a better life than mine and to do so, you need to have a good education. No one can help you but yourself. So try, won't you dear, to get good results in your exams it will mean so much to you in the end.

And perhaps I was beginning to take notice of Vic's comments on my conduct report: 'Barbara should pay more attention to her work and not be so easily led into mischief!' For I was soon writing to Mother:

> Talking of spare time. My form mistress (Miss Newham) has definitely told me I'll have no spare time whatsoever, so now I know—told quite frankly! I am doing art as an extra and I

am having only two lessons a week, it looks as though my art mistress thinks I can get through school cert (Cambridge School Certificate). Well, I hope she is right.

I have often wondered how I would have managed to fit the practice and theory required into my time table, if I had been taking my music exams as well. Yes, work beckoned and although we were all in Dormitory One, we had not completely abandoned our desire to do the forbidden.

For several years, we had talked about organising a midnight feast. Well, that is what you did at a boarding school after all. And it was always written about in girls' comics, which of course we were not allowed to have, there were no teen magazines then. We had already tried to have some kind of feast, not during the night but just after tea, when we were in the first and second years.

In the Dining Hall, the Prefects, Sub–Prefects and Seniors sat at the ends of the tables, with everyone else in descending year order. Our plan was to secretly hide slices of bread in our napkins during the meal and somehow manage to take them out of the Hall. This was just for the sake of eating them in another place, which we were forbidden to do. At that particular tea, we had watercress and bread.

Surreptitiously we thought, we had managed to put quite a lot of so called, 'watercress sandwiches' inside our napkins, but we had not counted on the beady eye of Gwen, the Prefect. After grace had been sung for the second time to end the meal, we were told to sit down again and produce the 'sandwiches' that we were attempting to hide. Onto our plates they had to go and we were told to eat them all! But of course, we had already had enough. Needless to say we were not at all hungry that evening and neither did we try the same trick again. Since we could not hoodwink the Prefects, we had to wait for the years to pass by. No, not until the time we were made Prefects, but until we became Seniors in the House. In order to organise these midnight feasts we needed to enlist the help of the third year girls, who were still assisting with the washing up after tea. I can still recall one of them rushing out of the kitchen and throwing us some bread (we should have been elsewhere) which we smuggled back to the House, climbing up the creaking, polished stairs to our dormitory.

By this stage of the war, the beds had returned to their normal positions round the outside of the room. I know that Tris was with me, for we were using her case as storage for all the food. How much we thought we could store I cannot imagine. We also had to bring back to the dormitory something to fill all these sandwiches. I remember distinctly tying to open a tin, which I had brought from home at the beginning of term, with the end of a knife and banging it with the heel of my shoe and I succeeded. It really is amazing what determination can accomplish!

Somehow, we had managed to save a little of our meagre ration of margarine and butter. One of the girls Diana, told us that she could only eat butter. "Oh yes," we said, "we will make you special sandwiches." You can be sure that although we made a 'special' pile for Diana, the filling was exactly the same as all the others.

How was all this going to be organised? Mrs Darnel's bedroom was next to our dormitory. The Head Prefect of the school and the Head Prefect of the House also slept in our dormitory. They had to be in a very deep sleep and not hear us or for that matter know what we were planning!

Dawn was able to get up at any time and so it was agreed. At the appointed hour, she crept around silently, waking each of us up. We then slid a pillow down the bed as if we were still in it. Did we really think Vic would be fooled if she had walked in? Still, we had not stopped to consider any of the negatives, at the time we thought it was a jolly good idea.

Someone hung a blanket over the windows of the dormitory

doors. Then we gathered silently in our dressing gowns and sat in a circle at the end of the room between two rows of beds. We each had a torch, so we could see all the 'marvellous' food we had managed to smuggle out of the dining room. I am sure that even though we tried to whisper, we must have giggled too, but somehow our Prefects slept serenely.

Oh yes, one more thing! We had devised an exit plan. In the event that Vic or Mrs Darnel appeared, we all had a nearby bed we were supposed to silently slide under, hoping we would not be heard or seen. But everybody in the dormitory, except us, carried on sleeping and we all crept back to our beds very pleased with ourselves that our plan had succeeded.

Did Vic ever know or guess? Sometimes I wonder—for shortly afterwards we were given a big surprise.

We went into the dormitory one evening to find figures in pyjamas stuffed and tied to the curtain rails and as we tried to get into bed, we discovered they had been made into 'apple pies!' These were quite a common prank that we used to play on each other, particularly when we were juniors. An 'apple pie bed' is one where the bedclothes have been re-arranged so that it is impossible to get into. Also, we often hid something prickly under the sheets, a hairbrush for example. And the legs and sleeves of pyjamas were tied in knots. It was a bit of fun, but also annoying as the bed had to be entirely remade.

But when we told some of the other girls in the school about the little joke, they were incredulous, not believing Vic was capable of playing such a trick on us, since they thought she had no sense of humour.

Now that we had moved up to the Senior Common Room, we had the wireless to listen to. I remember hurrying back for Winston Churchill's messages to the nation. We used to all gather round to hear him speak. And there was music too. We would dance to the new sounds. My cousin Ivor had taught me to Jitterbug during one of his visits to Worcester Park before the war, and because I liked dancing, I remember Tris and myself working out quite a good routine between the two of us.

On June 5, 1944, the sound of planes had intensified so it seemed to me, continuing all through the night. I recall clearly hearing wave after wave of planes flying over the school. So it was no real surprise to learn from the wireless the next morning that D–Day had finally arrived.

D–Day brought with it a lot of hope that the war might at last be coming to an end. But it also brought something else as a consequence of the Nazi's last ditch efforts to avoid defeat; the arrival of the V1 (doodle bugs as they were known) and V2 rockets. These were very frightening. Somehow I think more so than hearing the sound of the enemy bombers, the guns and the bombs exploding. The V1 engines droned at an unpleasant pitch and when they cut out, as they eventually did, there was no way of knowing where the bombs might land. Sometimes they just dropped straight down, like stones falling from the sky. Other times they would glide to earth before exploding. At least when we heard the engine stop, there was often enough time to run to a shelter. The V1s were called 'doodlebugs' as they flew straight and not so fast, they 'doodled' along and could be attacked by aircraft and the guns on the ground. Even though many were destroyed in this way, many more landed on London killing thousands of people and causing considerable damage to property.

I remember practising at school for an emergency, if for some reason we could not get to the trenches. We were expected to lie face down on the floor, hands covering our eyes, thumbs in ears. I do not suppose this would have helped very much, but maybe it would have lessened possible injuries, rather than if we had remained sitting at our desks.

For Mother who was working in the heart of London, it was a different matter. She was under constant threat from the 'flying bombs.' Always listening, always hoping they would not land near her. And always anxious, not knowing in which direction to run. Once the engines stopped they simply came out of the sky much faster than you would have expected; something we were both to learn from first hand experience.

I was home during the summer holidays. At about six o'clock one evening, just as Mother had arrived back from work in an air raid, we heard a flying bomb overhead. Then its engine cut out. We both dived for the Morrison shelter in the dining room, while the bomb swooshed to the ground and exploded in Windsor Road, not far away from our house.

We were a bit shaken as it had been so close. Then we looked at each other and realised that only our heads had made it under the cover of the shelter—the rest of us was still exposed, and extremely vulnerable to injury! Later we laughed about the episode. But the bomb in Windsor Road contributed to Mother's claim for war damage. She had to report all incidents following the first blast in 1941.

After this near miss, Mother decided it would be safer for me to spend the rest of the holiday with one of Father's sisters and her family in Plymouth. But Mother still had to remain in London and face the bombs. This was difficult, especially as she was now on her own at home. And matters were made worse in September 1944, when the V2 rockets arrived. These were far more frightening because there was no advance warning sound. They just landed and exploded. They were also more difficult for the gun batteries to hit. In fact there was no effective defence against them.

I think it was ultimately the V2 rockets and the constant anxiety of listening and wondering, "Where are they going to fall next?" that finally made Mother extremely stressed.

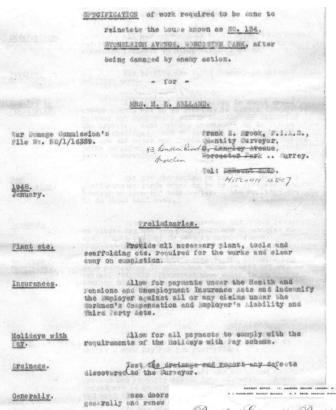

ABOVE: the surveyor's report itemising the repair work on Mother's house. RIGHT: the letter from the building society.

Back at school I was settling down to work and had heeded the advice of Mother and Miss Vickridge. I tried very hard to improve my work for the coming school certificate exams. We used to devise methods for helping each other revise. In subjects such as English Literature I often saw two girls walking round with the set text book, testing each other for quotations. The first question on the literature paper was always a quotation. It was worth learning as much as possible in order to get full marks here.

In my year, we were studying Hamlet and our teacher took us to London to see it performed on stage—a marvellous way of getting to know the play. This would have been quite a treat then. And air raids had probably lessened as the Allies were advancing in Europe.

Our external school exams were held in the gym. A member of staff sat at each end of the room invigilating. Carpet was laid between the rows of desks so that there was no noise whatsoever in the room. The gym was away from the classroom area and there was no disturbance by pupils passing the windows either. We were there on our own, with little mascots and clocks on our desks.

I seemed to manage most of the exams all right until it came to physics. We had to choose between science and Latin in the Fourth Year and I had opted for science. In those days the subject was made up of physics, chemistry and biology and I could at least draw and enjoyed biology. But the other two sciences really remained foreign languages to me. I might as well have been studying Latin, only I did not like the teacher!

When the exam came around, I sat looking at the questions and did not understand them at all. My answer paper went in with just my number on it. I have since learned that I was in good company, for apparently Winston Churchill had handed in a blank sheet for one of his exams when he was at Harrow. And I think I am right in quoting Nigella Lawson upon being given her 11+ arithmetic paper, she stood up, took it to the member of staff who was invigilating and said, "I don't do this subject." I would not have had Nigella's nerve, but I know exactly how she felt and I have often wondered what her father thought later, when he became Chancellor of the Exchequer.

And what happened about the results? We had the excruciating experience of having to sit on the floor, with the rest of the school in the Assembly Hall while Miss Fryer read them out. There was no receiving them in the privacy of our homes in an envelope. This was far worse than having our average weekly grades read out in front of the rest of the form.

In the Upper V, Miss Fryer would come into the classroom and as each girl's name was called, we were required to stand beside our desks whilst we heard our average grade for the week. The grades we received for each subject were handed into the form mistress, who calculated the final mark. We tried to know our grade by keeping our own account, but this was not always possible for every subject. Miss Fryer usually managed to make some comment to each of us. We always hoped it would be one of encouragement!

By now it was 1945, and events in the world had shifted dramatically. The war in Europe was drawing to a close. It had been nearly a year since D–Day and on June 5, we heard that hostilities had finally ceased. Here is the letter I wrote to Mother a few days later:

Sunday.
My darling Mummy,
Peace! Peace! Isn't it marvellous? What did you do on VE Day? On Monday when we heard the news flash, we dashed outside and danced and shouted around the 'Garth' and the large oak tree. On Tuesday morning we went to Chapel where we had a service, then we went swimming in House order. In the afternoon we

went out of bounds to collect wood for a large bonfire, which we were to have in the evening in the long grass by the hockey pitch. After listening to the King's speech at nine o'clock, we went down to the bonfire! It was fairly big, and the gardeners had been making it up all the afternoon. Though they said that if they had known before, the bonfire would have been much bigger.

At about ten to ten the bonfire was lit. The whole school was down, including the Weybridge lot. Then we proceeded to dance round it, shouting our hearts out. The bonfire was lovely. It was terribly bright. We went up to the Hall at eleven o'clock and left the bonfire still burning. We danced in the Hall for three dances. But when we got back to the House we did not go straight up to bed like the rest of the Houses. At last we put out the lights, and then we all got out of bed again and hung out of the windows in our pyjamas, watching the search-lights and fireworks. At about half past twelve we went to sleep.

On Wednesday we got up at half past seven in the morning. We had Victory Sports. I was in the obstacle race and we had to dress up. We had to jump in a sack, with a coat and awful old fashioned bathing cap on and hold an umbrella in one hand and in the other a satchel and the sack. There was a staff obstacle race and Vic won it. She did look funny. Everybody was most amused.

In the afternoon there were sports in the swimming bath, carried out by special girls. It was ever so good. Our House had made hats and in the evening we wore them to the party we had in the Hall. I am keeping mine as a souvenir. I will show it to you when you come, and please will you come on the 18th June. I think it is a Saturday. Please excuse writing as I am doing this outside the House, because it is such a lovely day.

Do you know that this is the first letter I have sent you in peace time for about six years! I have written to my man in the Merchant Navy, four pages which is not too bad. I did not want to write to the 1st, 2nd or 3rd engineer. I wanted to write to someone young. At least a 4th engineer should be fairly young and I certainly didn't want to write to anyone old. By the way, I forgot to tell you that we had a picnic on Wednesday. Each House went out by itself in the grounds, though we weren't allowed to go out of bounds.

Well Mummy, I must close now. All my love and please try to get a spool for my camera.

Lots of love and kisses from your loving little daughter,
Barbara.

I was so pleased to find this letter, it was not in an envelope and was written on thin paper. So it is now very fragile. What an important letter to write in pencil! I can remember the bonfire, making a hat and going to the Hall but not the rest of the week.

Neither do I recall writing to the 4th engineer. I wonder who he was? This was not to be the only hat I made during that summer of 1945.

By August, the end of the war in the Far East was announced. The Japanese had surrendered to the Americans after two terrible atomic bombs were dropped, one on Hiroshima and the other on Nagasaki. I was at home for the summer holidays and of course there was only one place to be on the day we celebrated the end of World War II and that was London.

Having already completed one hat, I spent the day making another very special one. We were planning to go to the capital with our neighbours and I wanted something different. I decided on a very tall Uncle Sam hat, but it had to be British as well. I painted red stripes on the main part and wanted to drape the Union Jack at the back from the crown to the brim. The Union flag that we had was too large, so Mother came up trumps as usual. She found in her dressing table drawer two crepe–de–chine scarves, printed with the flags of four nations. Incredibly they were, Britain, France, Germany and Japan.

She had kept them since the end of the First World War. I was so pleased. I shaped and stitched them to my hat. I do not recall the journey to or from London, but I do remember that we joined in with the crowds. There was no traffic, just throngs of people on the streets of the capital. They were singing and dancing, joining in together and all of us were heading for Buckingham Palace.

Mother was concerned about my safety and insisted that I linked arms with the two men in our little party. And so I was escorted down the centre of the Mall. Just as well, for everywhere we went I was often met with sailors singing to me, "Where did you get that hat?" an old London cockney song. We joined in the throng of people outside the palace gates, chanting, "We want the King! We want the King!" Naturally when the King and Queen accompanied by the two Princesses appeared on the balcony with Winston Churchill, everyone waved and cheered. After a while, we made our way back up the Mall and into Leicester Square. It was whilst I was joining in the Congo, that someone in the crowd thought they would punch my hat in. I felt a bang on the top of my head, but the hat did not crumple and bend, it remained in shape, probably helped by the two little scarves. I have treasured them ever since.

So World War II had finally ended. Millions of people had lost their lives and millions more had suffered unimaginably. The full horrors of Nazi and Japanese atrocities were yet to be disclosed to the world. And quite suddenly people had to adjust

LEFT: the Zetland group making silly poses!

RIGHT: a mixed group of juniors and seniors with the House Matron, Mrs Darnell.

to living in peace time again. But there would be no returning to life as it had been in 1939, everything had changed and a new era was beginning.

A new era was beginning for me too, back at school in September 1945. I had somehow managed to pass the requisite number of exams in School Certificate and now entered the Lower VI. A few of my friends had left school at sixteen and I had to face the decision of what I was going to do. In what direction would I go?

Of all the times that Mother had made the journey to visit me, from that first October in 1936, the two I remember most were in 1943 when she told me that Grandmother had died and in 1945 when we walked beneath the row of chestnut trees, discussing what my future career path should be. It was Mother who persuaded me that I should try to become a teacher. Looking back over her own experience of life, it is easy to understand why.

AFTER THE WAR
1945−47

I began what was to become my last year as a pupil at the Masonic School. I started my studies for the Higher School Certificate in the Lower VI. I knew that I would not be chosen for university, only the very clever girls were allowed to go and understandably the Masons had to be sure that they would complete the course satisfactorily. After all, they were paying for us, whichever college we attended.

But before then, I was given quite a difficult task. The Headmistress's birthday was approaching and someone decided that the school should give her a pair of leather gloves. As I liked gloves, I had the honour of making them and there was an excellent pattern at school. So I looked forward to doing this— that was until I saw the leather. It was beautiful, the finest suede in a pale aubergine colour (I have never forgotten it), every single finger touch was liable to leave a mark, I had to be incredibly careful not to be too heavy handed.

And I had a very responsible job, realising it was a privilege to have been asked. They turned out to be beautiful gloves, all the fingers had fine gussets on each side of them and they were so delicately shaped, that once completed they literally did fit the hand like a glove. Miss Fryer was delighted with her present and thanked the school at the end of prayers. All eyes turned towards me as the girls knew I was the pupil who had made them. Good practice for someone hoping to become a teacher to have everyone looking at you! Later in the same year, I was given the prize for handwork.

It was during this time in the Lower Sixth, that I had to make a choice, which I think now affected my future career. There must have been a period allocated on the timetable for when we were free to choose an activity.

I remember clearly standing in the corridor outside the art and handwork rooms. They were at right angles to each other. Looking into the art room on my right I saw a still life laid out with a stone jar. There were easels and I knew the girls were going to learn how to paint in oils. (Many years before, at the beginning of the war, Mother obtained through her brother Uncle Frank, who was an illustrator, oil paints, brushes and a palette for me. I had wanted an easel as well, but obviously it was much too expensive at the time. I had to wait until I was in my sixties before I eventually got one).

I did so want to go into the art room and learn to paint properly, but handwork also beckoned. For in a small section of the main classroom, I knew there was a potter's wheel. This was my other passion, as the French would say—I loved making pots. I turned left and my fate was sealed. Instead had I turned right, I am sure I would have gone to art college, which was really my rightful direction. As it was, my choice to pursue handwork led me down a route to a teacher training college with no specialist art department. But that was still in the future.

It was customary for Masonic girls going into either the nursing or teaching professions to spend a year in the Sanatorium or with the Weybridge children. But only two girls were selected in each case. So it was decided that instead of remaining in the Upper VI, when the time came, I would go back to Weybridge.

With the end of hostilities in Europe and Japan and no more

threats from flying bombs, life began to get back to normal, though rationing was to continue in Britain until 1954. School routines remained the same, but there were no longer any more interruptions—we did not have to leave suddenly and go down to the trenches during meal times. The few of us who remained from our large group were now Prefects in the House and we all had serious work to prepare for our exams.

The staff too must have felt that a great responsibility had been lifted from their shoulders. Looking after 400 girls was enough, without the added dangers imposed by a world war. They too needed some light relief at the end of what must have been six very fraught years and so they had planned an end of war celebration.

We were told to make our way over to the Assembly Hall. When we got there we found all the chairs were arranged in rows facing the stage. The curtains were closed. Not one of us had any idea why we were there or what was about to happen.

As silence settled on the excited group of girls, the curtains opened. There on the stage, standing still with not a muscle moving, looking straight ahead up to the balcony, stood immaculately dressed Roman soldiers—our teaching staff! This was the opening scene of '1066 And All That,' and dear Miss Funnell was at the front of the stage, immobile like a statue.

There might have been a hushed silence before the curtains parted but it did not last for long. All 400 of us erupted, producing the loudest burst of laughter that had ever been heard in the Hall! I am sure the decibel count would have made interesting reading.

What fun the staff must have had rehearsing for the play. How splendidly they performed it for us and all the preparations were done with such secrecy. Emboldened by this success, it was not long before they performed another play, this time of their own making, 'What Happened During The War?' No, that was not its title for I do not recall whether there had been one, but it was about memories of wartime at Rickmansworth, as seen from the teaching staff's point of view. My one abiding memory was the scene from the trenches. This was at the beginning of the war when the juniors were sleeping there. The staff however got very little sleep, even though they had their own mattresses on the duckboards. They spent their nights picking up the juniors as we fell off the benches. As I had been one of them, this was the first time I realised what life had been like for our teachers—a little eye opener, so to speak.

It was decided I would take the Higher Certificate in the July of 1946 and I was chosen as one of the two pupil teachers going to Weybridge. By September of that year, the Weybridge girls returned to their junior school and I went with them. What an exciting prospect lay in store for me, but before then there was another event full of expectation.

During the last year of a girl's life at Rickmansworth, she was summoned over to the main administration block. There she would discuss with Matron, the clothes she would like to have on leaving the school.

Measurements were taken and we had to rely entirely on Matron's choice for us and remember rationing was still in force. I was fortunate, in that the Head Matron was now Miss Wade. Yes, the same Miss Wade who had nicknamed me Kelly on my first night at Weybridge in 1936.

We were allowed a choice of two garments from a coat, a dress or a suit. They were called costumes then. I had lived in a dress for the last ten years and so I chose a suit and I asked for two. A good selection really as I was hoping to go on to teacher training college and a suit would have been the most sensible garment for me to wear. We were also given sufficient fabric to make ourselves two pairs of pyjamas. So it was off to the needlework room and Miss Atherton, though by now I was quite capable of following a pattern and knew how to insert sleeves and put on a collar. We waited very excitedly for the telephone call, summoning us over to Miss Wade's office.

I was delighted with her choice for me, or perhaps I was allowed to select from several garments. Anyway, I ended up with a French blue woollen winter suit and an olive green suit with gold trimmings and short sleeves in a moygashel fabric for summer. Both colours were just right for me, especially as my hair had started to return to its original colour of dark chestnut. I remember wearing these garments years later, even though Dior and his New Look were to revolutionise our fashions in 1947.

The generosity of the Masons was completed with a dozen white linen handkerchiefs, a Bible and prayer book. There was a print of the beautiful alter and choir stalls in the Chapel at the front of both. They were signed by the Chairman of the House Committee at that time. I was deemed to have left the school, even though I would go back to the Junior School for another year.

In September 1946, I made the journey not to Baker Street and Rickmansworth, but to Waterloo and then Weybridge. Because I was judged to be 'on the staff' at the start of term, I returned before the pupils. I knew where I was going, but for the little girls who had been at Rickmansworth during the war, a great change awaited them.

They would join a much smaller school and grounds. There would only be 120 of them instead of another 400 they had grown used to. They would also be leaving Miss Mildred Harrop, who was to retire as Headmistress and instead, Miss Isobel Vaughan would take over the post as Head of the school.

She was not a stranger to them. An old girl herself, it was Miss Vaughan who had taught me at Weybridge and in whose form room I had looked longingly out of the window at the beautiful delphiniums. Neither were other staff strangers. Back to Weybridge went the Head Matron Miss Dunn, together with Miss

Amy Page, Miss Margaret Moore and Miss Stella Keyes. I have no recollection of the other teachers—but Ivy was still there, wheeling the staff trolley from the kitchen through the school to the staff dining room, where I would now be taking my meals.

I had looked forward to returning to Weybridge. I was back as a pupil teacher, supporting the other staff and responsible for taking care of the children during the day. I helped every evening at bedtime to supervise the bathing and washing routines and generally settled the girls down in the dormitories. I can recall doing a lot of my duties in the new wing, perhaps because these dormitories were in an area of Weybridge where I had not gone as a pupil.

Of course I was not on duty all the time and on my free days I could go out of school—by myself! I was allowed to walk anywhere in the grounds, to all those areas that had previously been out of bounds for me. One day, early in that September before the girls had arrived back, Miss Dunn asked me to cut some flowers from the garden and make two floral arrangements for the fireplaces in the dining room. I was absolutely delighted she had given me this task to do and went off happily, to search for suitable foliage.

In a section of the kitchen gardens I found some beautiful feathery fern, which was just what I wanted as a contrast to the rest of my armful of flowers and leaves. I had completed one of the arrangements and was feeling very satisfied with the result, when to my dismay I heard a familiar voice behind me, filled with disapproval. I had picked the asparagus fern and Miss Dunn was not in the least bit pleased!

How was I to know? I had never eaten asparagus never mind seen it growing. However, I would not make the same mistake twice and anytime I see asparagus now, my mind always goes back to that first encounter with it.

Mother now had the problem of providing me with clothes, for I was no longer wearing school uniform. No wonder the LCC had wanted her to teach in their make do and mend wartime classes. She remodelled and made me a splendid little wardrobe. Many of the garments were literally assembled from pieces, patterns matched and put together, but only the two of us would know this, not the rest of the world. These clothes would later be worn when I went to college.

I knew that the pupil teachers at Weybridge had a little bedroom of their own. I asked if I could have the room (it had been my duty to clean when I was only eight years old), between Dormitories Four and Five. My request was granted and I was absolutely delighted.

This time the room was mine and I did not have to share it with anyone else. There was just sufficient space for a single bed, and on the opposite wall a chest of drawers and small wardrobe. Beside the bed was a window and I placed a chair underneath it. Because the room was next to Dormitory Four, I had a lovely view over the lawn again, and down to the rose arch. But best of all, an iron spiral staircase now wound its way up to the window, shrouded by a vine and on clear nights, the full moon shone into the room. Only seventeen years old at the time, I thought this was so romantic.

And at long last I had made it to the top two form rooms that led off the Common Room. It was here that I helped out a lot with all the handwork and learnt to card wool and then spin it. I did this by simply standing up, holding the spindle in front of me and giving it a twist so that it spun round like a top. I prepared the wool by teasing it out between my fingers. I mastered this quite easily and it was a skill that was to always stay with me.

I was fortunate to go on a weekend craft course later in my career and had the chance of learning to spin on a wheel, which I found such a relaxing thing to do. Though if I had to earn my living that way, I wonder if I would have enjoyed it as much.

In order to continue my studies in art and craft, I went to Chertsey Grammar School to join one of the senior art classes. It was a good experience for me to sample a small part of what life was like in other schools. I cannot remember being very impressed at all. In fact, nowhere would I find a place that came close to matching the standards set at the Masonic School.

While at Weybridge as a pupil, I had enjoyed working with raffia and string and rope, making Indian type baskets. So I now set about making a large basket using cane and raffia. The cane was very thick, strong and long and coiled around me as I sat in the middle of the pupil teacher's sitting room struggling to control it. Yes, the same little room where years before I had practised the dulcimer playing, 'Poor Old Joe' to the distraction of Miss Dunn who was in the room above!

But it was not just the art and crafts that I continued with. I also returned to my music. Miss Amy Page must have been the most talented teacher ever. Not only was she an accomplished musician herself, but she was blessed with understanding and patience. For she decided to take back this obstinate pupil and patiently encouraged me to play the piano again. How she managed to achieve this I shall never know, but she allowed me to experience music in a way that I have never forgotten.

Looking back it has always seemed remarkable to me that having stopped learning to play at fourteen years old, I was able to start again at seventeen and reach a standard that enabled me to study music as one of my subjects at teacher training college.

This was entirely due to Miss Page and I owe her a tremendous debt of gratitude. It was not too long before I was playing Chopin, Beethoven and Grieg. It is the Grieg 'Wedding March' that I remember mostly, for I was able to learn this off by heart and had the added joy of being allowed to play on the baby grand piano in the staff dining room.

It was a beautiful, oak panelled room, like the school Dining Hall, with a large circular dining table in the centre and over by the casement window, the piano. It was not black, like the ones at Rickmansworth, but toned in with the rest of the wood in the room. My abiding memory from this time, which has remained all my life, is sitting playing the piano, with the casement window slightly open and the scents of the garden wafting in. I assumed I was playing this particular piece of music to a reasonable standard—until that illusion was cruelly shattered many decades later when I heard it played by a professional pianist and realised my short comings—ignorance is bliss as they say!

Of short comings, there were many. Miss Page wanted me to play for the school prayers. Assembly as it is now called. She chose a simple piece of music and I practised hard until I knew it off by heart. Then the dreaded day came when Miss Page was to take evening prayers and I would play the hymn. All started well until I hit a wrong note. I was lost. I sat with my hands in my lap looking sadly at the hymn book before me on the piano. Miss Page proudly sang with all the little girls. I felt so stupid and embarrassed to have let her down—again.

But there was never a rebuke, only more encouragement. Somehow, I managed during my school practice later at college, to play for the music singing lessons. Looking back it appears to me now as nothing short of a miracle that I did so.

Towards the end of 1946, the senior school at Rickmansworth was preparing for an important event. King George VI and Queen Elizabeth were coming to visit. The girls of course would perform the School Drill. I thought it was rather nice that Eileen, the other pupil teacher and myself had been invited to return to Rickmansworth to join in the practice sessions and take our places with the other girls.

Although the PE member of staff stood on the side just above the piano, played by a music teacher, it was Miss Fryer who took command, walking between the rows correcting any arm, head, or leg that was not in exactly the same position as the girl in front, for we were to look as one. Neither was a single hair to come out of place, it was not to move! When heads had to bend down in certain movements our hair had to remain perfect, no hanging over our faces. Oh, no, Miss Fryer was having none of that, stray hair was kept firmly in place. We must have looked a strange sight, with so many hair grips all over our heads. Those of us with fine, fly away hair, gave the impression we were wearing some kind of odd helmet.

And smiles—no smiles as Miss Fryer called them. You may be wondering what on earth she meant? She was referring to the gaps between our knicker legs and the tops of our stockings!

"The King does not want to see smiles," she declared as she went round the Hall inspecting us. I know this for a fact as she was standing near me as we performed the movement where we had to bend over. In the fog of the passing years, Miss Fryer's comment has always puzzled me. Surely we would not be bending over with our backs to the King and Queen sitting on the stage? I have never solved the puzzle.

Eileen and I would have travelled to Rickmansworth with Miss Keyes, who owned a car. School Drill was practised in the morning and so we were there to join in. Later that day in the afternoon, the King and Queen were scheduled to visit and stay for tea. I can only recall from memory, that the drill went well as usual. Then after we finished tea, we lined up between the trees on the main drive, to cheer the King and Queen as they left in their limousine.

Now my turn had come to leave. It was winter time and the weather was as unpredictable as ever. A thick fog had descended all around. I remember the journey back to Weybridge very clearly, particularly as Miss Keyes was driving and this would have been one of the few times I had travelled by car. I was not used to it at all, unlike children are today, so for me it would have seemed like a treat. But it did not turn out that way! I sat in the front passenger seat, half hanging out of the car in order to guide

Miss Keyes back to school. The fog was so thick, it became impossible for her to see the side of the road—that was my job. So with me calling out directions, we slowly made the return journey to Weybridge. It was just as well in those early days of motoring that there were so few vehicles on the road.

Summer time had arrived and I now enjoyed walking along the riverbank, watching the boats at the rowing club, sitting on the green opposite the school, where the local cricket team played at the weekends and as a seventeen going on eighteen year old, I used to day dream.

One of my dreams was to own a pair of sandals—white ones. Miss Keyes had some and I was very intrigued by them. Having lived in the company of women for so many years, I had not been aware of their clothing sense or their shoes, except for Miss Atherton and Lady Harris, who always sat on the stage on Committee Days. I had noticed she wore what would have been fine silk stockings—the Americans had not yet arrived with their 'nylons.' Miss Keyes's sandals were something different and I longed to have my own pair and they had to be white. To save enough money to buy them was totally out of the question. As a pupil teacher, I earned just a few shillings a month and it would have taken me years to save up. No, I had to find another way if I was to fulfil my little dream.

There was a Woolworth's in Weybridge then, as there was in nearly every small town in the 1930s. And it was to Woolworth's I went on my search. I had by now worked out how I could make a pair of sandals, not from leather of course but from canvas webbing. I knew I could find soles, because we had all made slippers in handwork. Surely if there were soles suitable for slippers, then I must have been able to find soles that would be passable, notice I have not said suitable because a leather sole would have been better. But I only needed something that would be strong enough to see me through the summer months of 1947.

So, my search at Woolworth's began and I was rewarded. I found soles and the white canvas webbing and another coloured webbing with which to make a matching summer handbag! Thrilled with my small and cheap purchases I returned up the hill to the school. I knew where I would go to machine all these narrow strips of canvas together—to the new wing linen room and the treadle machine there. So began the task of making the sandals and the handbag. The white canvas I folded in half lengthwise, this made a strip just over half an inch wide. This was machined on the edge down both sides. The sole I had chosen was quite deep and a strip of this canvas fitted nicely all round the edge, I had made up a design for the canvas to crossover my feet and these strips were sewn on first. But how was I to fasten the sandals and how was I going to keep them on? I managed somehow to work out a system with a piece of canvas fitting round the back of my heel to be secured with a hook and bar eye—elastic and buckle would have cost more money and 'Velcro' had yet to be invented.

All I had to do now was to whiten the canvas. We were used to wearing white plimsoles for all our summer activities and these had to be kept clean. No trainers then, no creams just to spread on. Instead, we had a hard white block of cleaning substance. This was moistened with a damp sponge, which was then applied to the shoe. It had to be done carefully, otherwise it would cause streaks and it had to be applied the night before I wanted to wear the sandals, so they would be dry by the morning.

The bag was no problem, it was just a matter of stitching strips of the canvas webbing together to form one piece of fabric folded over with a strong white zip to fasten it, plus a handle made from double webbing. I was very proud walking out in my sandals (that usually goes before a fall), carrying my summer hand bag. I had at last managed to leave the black shoes behind, for a few hours each week. They just lasted the summer, which was all I was expecting really—but the bag? Ah, that remained with me for decades and when eventually I had a home of my own, it became my clothes peg bag and was only discarded relatively recently.

I now realise, that having the freedom to walk in the beautiful Surrey countryside was a real privilege, something that today would be considered too risky for a young woman or child to do alone. I revelled in the beautiful scenery around me. The memories of the acres of rhododendrons, silver birch and pine trees have remained with me constantly and provide the yardstick by which I have measured my surroundings through-out my life. And for me, nowhere has ever surpassed Surrey.

Mother still came to visit me as she had done for nearly eleven years. Now when we went out together, it was to go for a special tea. Those were the days before coffee shops and fast food outlets. Instead, there were little tea rooms privately owned, each with their own individuality. One near the village green at Rickmansworth served not only tea and cakes but sold what we would now call bric–a–brac. Best of all they had 'Kunzle' cakes. These were made by a national company and each one was differ-ent. They were small, about the size of a mince pie and often quite elaborate examples of the confectioner's art. They all tasted delicious and I liked their decoration and design. One small cake I recall was made from thin squares of dark chocolate forming a box shape around a delicious cream centre (of some kind). These cakes were expensive for us and so were a treat to savour and remember.

Following the end of hostilities, the men and women who had served in the armed forces were being gradually demobbed and returned to 'civvy street.' At about this time, I was applying for a place at teacher training college. Although there was a teacher shortage, ex-service people were given priority over other applicants, which made things more difficult for me. My case was not helped either by the fact they had a greater experience of life. They had not just gone from school, to college and back to school as I had done. I have always thought that teachers need a wider experience of things outside of school, in order to make them more effective in the classroom. Many of the former service personnel now wanted their old jobs back and this of course had an impact on Mother's position on the railway. Her job as Welfare Officer was no longer required, the women were expected to leave and make way for the men.

Fortunately for Mother, unemployment was not about to strike for a third time. She was able to stay in administration, and got a new job at one of Southern Railways' offices at Waterloo, which was to see her through to retirement. When she arrived at the station, she did not have very far to travel, just a short walk from one end of the concourse to the other, where the office was located. She had enjoyed her teaching days at Bloomsbury Trade School, but I am sure she missed that environment, though she was still able to keep in touch with teacher friends, as they lived near us in Surrey.

I was a grateful recipient yet again, of a garment made at Bloomsbury. The tailoring mistress had made me a lovely dressing grown when I went off to Weybridge and later she was to make a very smart suit for me when I started college. This was commented on by the college principal, when she wrote my report from my final school practice.

Mother also had to readjust to peace time. This was the second of two major wars she had experienced in her life. During the first, she was a teenager writing to young men on the front line. There were three from Waterloo who she had kept in contact with, and they continued their correspondence even after one of them had emigrated to Canada. They always exchanged long and interesting letters every Christmas. At the end of World War II she was in her forties and faced making one more difficult adjustment to her life, knowing she still had another twenty years before retirement.

One of the joys at the end of hostilities was being able to visit Ireland again. This we did with a great sense of expectation, particularly Southern Ireland, since it had the most delicious food and had never been subject to rationing. In England however, rationing continued well after the war ended. Although it was something we had grown used to, this did not necessarily mean everybody readily accepted it.

Mother liked to recall an incident which she had heard about when she was working at the railway depot. A group of women had decided to smuggle butter back to England. Our butter ration had only been two to four ounces per person per week, and the thought of having unlimited supplies must have been very tempting.

For some considerable time, the slim English women made the journey from Holyhead to Dun Laoghaire returning with much fuller figures. After a while, a keen eyed customs officer realised he recognised these women. How slim they had been a few weeks earlier and how much weight they had mysteriously gained on their return. And so a plan was put into action.

One day, the same women were seen yet again making the journey to Ireland. When they returned, they appeared at the customs check point with nicely rounded figures. Custom officials asked them to step inside their office. A roaring fire had been made and the women were told to wait. Their discomfort soon became obvious. They miraculously lost all those extra pounds and with the sight of rivers of melted butter gathering at their feet, there was no need for any questions and little point in denying what they had been trying to do.

With my Grandparents now dead, Mother and I had the little house to ourselves. Our living room upstairs, where Mother had worked so hard and continuously on the treadle machine, became my bedroom. The garden had now matured in the 'rustique' way as the French say. The trellis had long been replaced, my swing under the archway had gone, but the roses still wound themselves over the new wooden supports.

Mother continued sewing, and I am sure she found this an outlet for her creative talents. The Southern Railways ran craft competitions between their employees and Mother enjoyed making her exquisite lingerie to enter in the embroidery section. She always won a little shield, for the standard of her work was

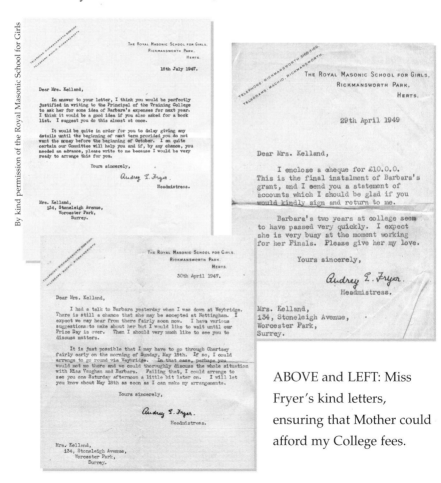

By kind permission of the Royal Masonic School for Girls

ABOVE and LEFT: Miss Fryer's kind letters, ensuring that Mother could afford my College fees.

quite exceptional. Not sewing during the day, gave her the opportunity in the evening, even if it sometimes meant she had to stand under the centre light in the living room to see more clearly!

By now I had successfully obtained a place at teacher training college. But unknown to me, a great deal of correspondence had taken place between Mother and Miss Fryer. I was astonished at the consideration and time that she had given to my situation. I am only sorry I was unaware of this interest earlier in my life. I would like to have spoken to her and thanked her properly. The Masons were paying my tuition and boarding fees during this period, and I had no idea that Miss Fryer had interceded on my behalf with the House Committee for support to be sent to Mother during the college holidays as well.

How could I not be filled with eternal gratitude for all the help and support Mother and I were given? Of course, we would never know the names of the individual Masons who contributed through their Lodges, but without their help and philanthropic spirit, our lives would have been very bleak.

Instead, I was enriched beyond measure and given the privilege of attending a school where I received an all round education, just as Mother had wanted, when she wrote in her diary of 1934 these words:

> I had made up my mind that when you were
> old enough, I should endeavour to get you into
> the Masonic School, where the education is the
> best in the land.

But had I been happy? A lot of happiness depends on an individual's personality. Certainly at Weybridge my letters, give the impression of a happy little girl, enjoying what the school had to offer and keeping busy with her friends. Even so, in nearly every letter I am counting the number of weeks and days until the end of term. As it drew to a close we would sing a little ditty to the tune of the 'Kempton Races.' It went like this:

> This time next week, where shall we be?
> Do dah dodah
> Not in this RMIG
> Da do dah day
> No more spiders in my bath
> Do dah dodah
> Trying to make me laugh
> Da do da day
> No more …

The next little verse was made up and so on. The sense of always looking forward to next week, remained a constant theme both at Weybridge and Rickmansworth.

And was I happy at the senior school? Well, adolescence and acne happened. I retreated within myself as anyone who has suffered with problem skin will appreciate. My acne was particularly severe, more so than other girls of my age and continued for all the years I was at school and on my return to Weybridge.

But I was not ignored and left to get on with it. At Rickmansworth, I was given yeast tablets to try to clear my skin. That might have helped a little, but the damage to me and my development as a person had already been done. Why did most of the other girls around me have no spots? Why had I not inherited my Mother's flawless skin? For flawless it was. She was blessed with a true peaches and cream complexion right into old age.

At one of the routine visits to our local doctor in Worcester Park, this was the obligatory medical examination before we returned to school at the end of a holiday, looking at my acne covered face, dear Dr Robinson asked, "How old are you now Barbara?" When I replied, "Seventeen," his response was, "Ah, kissable age."

Further action to help me was duly taken. When I returned to Weybridge as a pupil teacher, I went to the local hospital for UVA treatment (this was the prescribed 'cure' for acne then). I clearly recall the sessions, and the resultant very red face, which came up by the evening. But that did not matter, as I was only helping the little ones with their bathing before bed. Everything was fine, until one session, when a young nurse appeared in the room and lowered the lamp even closer to my face. The result this time was a severe case of sun stroke and sun burn. Not only was my face flaming red, I was also very ill. The sessions were stopped immediately, and it would only be later in life that the final impact of this treatment manifested itself, in the form of premature skin damage.

However, that day was a long way off and I am sure that the treatments helped give me the confidence I needed to be more self assured.

A fter the long years of war there were many shortages, and clothing parcels were sent from kind Americans. I was very fortunate to receive two items, because a private client of Mother's had connections in America.

I was given a butter yellow pigskin coat and a black gross grain evening top, which fastened with two large golden buttons. These garments formed part of my small wardrobe as I went off to college. The pigskin coat was a marvellous example of tailoring, with a blouson back bodice, long revers (so I always needed a scarf) and wide shoulders. This was typical war time style. There were deep side pockets and a belt, which was the only area that showed any signs of wear so I had to compromise here with another belt. My college scarf proved ideal as the colours were a black and gold stripe on a very dark green background. It was the ideal complement. I wore them both gratefully.

The pigskin coat could not have come at a better time, for 1947 saw Britain in the grip of a very severe winter. The black gross grain top fitted me perfectly. It had a square neck line and three quarter length sleeves. It was like a semi–jacket really and at least I had something to wear, with a simple taffeta skirt from C&A on Oxford Street, for the all important college dances.

The label inside the pigskin coat read, 'Fifth Avenue, New York.' I thought that was great, and felt I should wear the coat inside out so everyone could see where it had come from! These extra garments were treats, as clothing was still rationed and had been since 1941. The government had made strenuous efforts to see that fabric of all kinds was used sparingly and had introduced a clothing scheme. The clothes made this way had to comply with strict regulations, regarding the length and number of pockets for example, in order to limit the amount of cloth used.

All these garments carried a utility mark—CC41, standing for Civilian Clothing 1941. Surprisingly these clothes were well made and they were cheaper than non–utility clothes, so eventually they found favour with consumers. They were also well designed, as top fashion designer such as Worth and Norman Hartnell were asked to submit their ideas for the style of the garments. Consumers became confident that these utility marked clothes were not only fashionable but good value for money. The introduction of such a scheme by the government meant that retailers were prevented from benefiting from clothes shortages and increasing their prices.

But in 1947, much to the dismay of some members of the government I am sure, Christian Dior introduced his 'New Look.' This was revolutionary, the design used much more fabric and women now had a feminine style, far removed from the square shouldered military inspired war time garments. I was one of the young women who rejoiced in having much nicer clothes to wear.

Along with the 'New Look' came American servicemen and 'nylons.' For someone who had to wear lisle stockings, these new garments were a revelation. Up until that time, the only fine stockings that women could get were made of silk. These were expensive and could not really compare with the fineness of nylon. Never mind that the Americans had chewing gum, ("Got any gum chum?" became the usual question people asked when they spotted an American in uniform), it was the nylons young women craved! And there were plenty to choose from, particularly on London's Oxford Street. Here we would find men selling packets of stockings out of suitcases on the pavement. Or standing in front of shop windows with a tray suspended from their necks. They would call out their wares as people passed, just like street traders always did, but they also kept an eye open for a policeman on his beat, for this type of trading was not allowed.

Of course there was a catch. These nylons were cheap or so they appeared, but I wonder how many women, when they returned home and opened up their purchases, discovered that their 'bargains' had two heels or no feet at all. Remember stockings still had a seam up the centre back and were shaped (tights did not appear until the 1960s, when the mini–skirt was introduced). So although it was great to have such a wide selection to choose from, we always had to take great care. Del Boy would have been in his element!

Towards the end of the summer term in 1947, I saw my school life turn full circle. I was leaving Weybridge, the very place where I had started my days at the Masonic School in 1936, aged only seven. Before term ended, I received one more privilege. I was given a ticket for a seat in the Albert Hall during the Promenade season in August—something I expect other Masonic girls who had achieved a certain standard of music also looked forward to in their time. I was very proud to sit in the hall and be part of the 'music scene.'

It might appear that I had sacrificed a lot, being sent away to a boarding school, knowing very little home life. But the opposite is true. As an only child with no other children of my age in the immediate family, I had grown up with many friends and in the company of other little girls, with all the trials, tribulations and joys experienced during childhood. I had become fiercely independent (very difficult to live with!) and extremely organised. Unfortunately, this habit tends to extend not only to the organisation of daily tasks, but to other people as well.

But there have also been compensations. I have some very close friends and we have remained in touch all these years. We do not see each other very often, as we are living far apart, but we remember birthdays and Christmas, and there is always the telephone to make sure we keep in touch. Jackie, my friendly rival in so many areas of our school life, continues to write and I can recall her face as vividly as if it were still that first day in September 1936.

I was enriched by my experiences at the Masonic School and look back with enormous gratitude at being given so many opportunities. I had lived a privileged existence, even with the restrictions imposed on us all during war time. It was Mother who had made the sacrifices, not me. She faced life alone and at times felt isolated. The closeness of the family had gone—another one of those unexpected consequences of the war. As Maisie her cousin wrote in a letter to me, (she was also on her own but based in Hertfordshire), 'If only we had all lived nearer, we could have helped each other more.' The cousins had all been so close throughout their childhood, living as young women in London. The coming of the war had split the family up, sending it to different parts of England.

But we had all survived. How many other families in Europe could have said the same thing?

EPILOGUE

FROM LEFT TO RIGHT: at the 1988 Bicentenary Old Girls' Reunion, June, me, Marie, Jackie and Pat.

RICKMANSWORTH, JUNE 1988

I was determined to make the effort to return to Rickmansworth one more time. It was June 1988 and the school was celebrating its bicentenary. 'Old Girls' went back to meet up with long lost friends and visit old haunts one more time.

And come they did, from all quarters of the globe. It was a magnificent effort, especially from those girls who had made new lives overseas. Nearly all the old crowd of Zetland had returned and it was great to meet up with them again to hear about how they were getting on in life and about their families. So much talking to be done! So many treasured photographs to be taken.

One thing I wanted to do was retrace my steps, and return to the areas that had meant so much to me as a pupil. I decided to make my way from Zetland House to the art department. This involved walking along the main classroom corridor. I was aware of being on my own, until I noticed a figure approaching from the opposite direction. And then we both stopped, held out our hands and in unison uttered the same name, "Margaret!"

The shadow cast by that day in July 1939 on the stage at Wigmore Hall had never left us. The other lady I had been reunited with was Olwen, the third member of our piano playing little trio.

PART TWO

I: CHEVALIER RUSPINI

II: A SHORT HISTORY OF THE ROYAL
MASONIC INSTITUTION FOR GIRLS

III: THE ADMISSION PROCEDURE, 1934–5

IV: A SHORT HISTORY OF FREEMASONRY

CHEVALIER RUSPINI:
FOUNDER OF THE SCHOOL

I: Chevalier Ruspini
The Dental Surgeon

Bartolomeo Ruspini was born near the town of Bergamo in Northern Italy in 1728. His father was Andrea Ruspini of Gramello, a descendant from an ancient family with contacts to many members of the nobility in Italy. Ruspini first trained as a surgeon in Bergamo completing his studies at the age of thirty six. He decided to specialise in dentistry and went to Paris, the recognised centre at the time. He worked under the dental surgeon to Louis XV.

Early in 1759, he moved to England and set up his own dental practice in Bath. He obtained letters of introduction from important noblemen, and he was most probably introduced to the Court of St James through letters from the Duke of Saxe–Gotha to the Dowager Princess of Wales, the mother of George III and Ruspini's patroness. Through these contacts he was able to enter the highest circles of English society, otherwise it would have been well nigh impossible for him to have achieved such a quick advance through the ranks of the highly stratified society of the period.

In 1766, he renounced the Catholic faith enabling him to marry for the second time. His bride was Elizabeth Ord and they married in St James's Piccadilly. She was a member of the wealthy and well connected Ord family who lived at Longbridge Hall, Berwick on Tweed. They had nine children, five girls and four boys.

Ruspini practised his profession at 32, St Albans Street, Pall Mall, where he made his own tinctures toothpastes, powders and brushes. He also began to market dental products across the country, which made up a considerable part of his business. In 1786, he published a pamphlet on his styptic—this is the medical term used to describe a preparation that constricts blood vessels and helps stop wounds bleeding. By 1791, Ruspini's styptic was in widespread use and highly praised by surgeons. It was credited with saving the life of the Prince of Wales in 1786 and the following year he was appointed as the Prince's dentist. The styptic was also adopted by the Royal Navy to stop excessive bleeding as it could be used for other parts of the body in addition to the mouth.

As one of his first publicised acts of benevolence, he ensured that his prescription was made available to the poor of London's East End free of charge. Life during the latter part of the eighteenth century was harsh. There were constant wars and not surprisingly many of Ruspini's contemporaries were more concerned with conviviality than with observing the teachings of the Masonic Craft.

During the Seven Years War (1756–1763) many Italians fled from oppressive French and Austrian armies and began to settle in England. In April 1789, Ruspini received the honour of the Chevalier of the Golden Spur, in recognition of his renowned benevolence and the opening of the first Masonic girls' school at Somer's East Place.

This honour was customarily given by the Pope, and in the light of Ruspini's conversion to the Anglican faith, his second marriage and the fact he was a Freemason, he seems a very unlikely candidate for the Pope's favours.

It has been suggested that it is the only known example of a papal honour being bestowed on someone with Ruspini's background. While there is no disputing he was given the honour, it seems unlikely it was granted by the Pope. A more plausible explanation suggests that it was in fact the Duke of Sforza–Cesarini who gave Ruspini the award, the Duke's ancestor having received the right to grant the honour from Pope Paul III in perpetuity.

In view of Ruspini's conversion from Catholicism and less than favourable opinion held by Rome towards Freemasonry, this explanation seems the most reasonable one. Though of course, it in no way diminishes the honour.

Ruspini died aged eighty six on December 14, 1813, and was buried in the churchyard of St James's, Piccadilly. Historians had tried to find his grave even before World War II started. Unfortunately during the Blitz, Piccadilly was badly bombed and much of the churchyard has been subsequently reconstructed, so Ruspini's final resting place is not known. His obituary in the 'Gentleman's Magazine' read:

> December 14, in Pall Mall aged 86, Surgeon Dentist to his R H the Prince Regent. The memory of the Chevalier will long be revered by his family and friends and his loss will be deeply deplored by the unfortunate, whom he had a habit of consoling and by the indigent whose wants he was ever ready to relieve. He was the founder of the most excellent Institution for the Support and Education of the Female Orphan Children of Free Masons.

The total value of his estate was less than £450. Although he would certainly have made a very good income as a dental surgeon he enjoyed at high standard of living in London—he lived in Pall Mall opposite Carlton House the residence of the Prince of Wales. Also, his many charitable commitments meant he had very little money left over to save.

Ruspini's eldest son inherited the business but he did not enjoy it for very long. Just fourteen years after his father's death in 1827, he petitioned his Lodge claiming he was in distress, caused by a mental breakdown. By an ironic twist of fate, the eldest son's two daughters attended the very school their grandfather had established.

Ruspini the Freemason

> 1762, initiated into a Lodge meeting at the Bush Tavern, Bristol No 116.
> 1769, joined Lodge of Emulation No 21.
> 1770, joined St Alban's Lodge No 29. Master in 1781.
> 1776, joined Lodge of Antiquity No 2.
> 1777, founder of the Lodge of the Nine Muses No 235.
> 1778, Master of the Royal Lodge, now Royal Alpha Lodge No 16.
> 1787, founder of the Prince of Wales Lodge No 259.
> 1788, joined Grand Masters Lodge No 1. Founder of the Royal Cumberland Girls' School 1791–1813, Grand Sword Bearer.

Ruspini became a Freemason when he was accepted into the Bush Lodge in Bristol in 1762. His first attempt in Bath, three years previously had proved unsuccessful. He was black balled and barred from reapplying for three months, though he never attempted to gain admission to that Lodge again. Over the course of his life, he had held office in eight different Lodges.

In 1777, he founded the Lodge of the Nine Muses. For the time, its furniture and jewels were far more beautiful and the workmanship of a much higher quality than anything that had so far been seen in Freemasonry. No doubt this was in part due to the large numbers of Italians in the Lodge, and their fine sense of aesthetic awareness.

Ruspini's Nine Muses was a success from the beginning and quickly attracted many distinguished aristocrats, past Grand Masters, foreign dignitaries and prominent figures from the arts world: Giovanni Cipriani, (Florentine artist), Francesco Bartolozzi (Florentine artist and engraver to George III), Johann Christof Bach (son of the composer Johann Sebastien). Early members also included three Ambassadors from Venice and one from Genoa. He was very keen to befriend foreigners and refugees many of whom had come from Italy and sought asylum in England.

Ten years later, on Ruspini's suggestion, the Prince of Wales established the Prince of Wales Lodge in 1787. It existed exclusively of people who had been given appointments by the Prince or were in some way closely connected with him. Ruspini was elected the first Treasurer and in 1791 the Grand Sword Bearer. Both positions he retained until his death. Members of the Prince of Wales Lodge were to play a leading role in the establishment of the first Masonic School in 1788. Of the eight special committee members who formulated the scheme for helping the daughters of Freemasons, six belonged to the Prince of Wales Lodge and the other two were prominent members of the Grand Lodge. Because of the way he was regarded in society, Ruspini was able to obtain the support and money from many London Masons. However, the school was not recommended to Freemasons throughout the country by the Grand Lodge until 1790, when the Duke of Cumberland died and the Prince of Wales took over as Grand Master and Patron of the school.

The original purpose of Ruspini in establishing the school was to safeguard the daughters of distressed Freemasons, while qualifying the girls with a useful skill—rather than the menial type of activity they might have expected would be their lot in life.

Ruspini was very much a man of his times. The eighteenth century was called the Age of Enlightenment, a period when scientists and philosophers argued for the creation of a better world, founded on the principles of democracy, a belief in individual rights, such as dignity, free speech and association and the right to follow any or no religion. On the big issues of the day, Ruspini was opposed to slavery and the coercion of the American colonists, just as he had been against French and Austrian domination of Italy.

By kind permission of the Royal Masonic School for Girls

The statue of Chevalier Ruspini, outside the Chapel at Rickmansworth. Every year on March 25, the school remembers its founder by celebrating Ruspini Day.

During his life, Ruspini was the target for all kinds of accusations and the subject of much gossip. This may have been caused by jealousy of his professional and social success, but he was also an Italian living in London. He would have brought with him a love of pageantry and display, qualities which may not have gone down so well with English society at the time. He also believed that the status of women should be improved. This must have seemed a radical idea for the age. While he had a positive impact on Masonic thought and actions during the latter part of the eighteenth century, he will be best remembered as the founder (he liked the title Institutor), of the Royal Masonic Institution for Girls.

A SHORT HISTORY OF
THE ROYAL MASONIC INSTITUTION
FOR GIRLS

II: The first Masonic school 1788–1795
Somers Place East, London

The first Masonic girls' school was founded on March 25, 1788 by Bartolomeo Ruspini and seven of his fellow Brothers. It was originally known as the Royal Cumberland Free Masons' School, after the patroness at the time, the Duchess of Cumberland. The Prince of Wales and the Dukes of Cumberland, Gloucester and York, all supported the project. Ruspini was appointed the first Treasurer, a post he held between 1788–1790.

The original address was at Somers Place East, which has since disappeared, but it was probably between the present Euston and St Pancras stations.

> 1) Qualifications for admission.
> Preference to be given to orphans, whose fathers at the time of their death were registered Freemasons and members of a Lodge. The first girls admitted had to be between the ages of five and ten. (This was later changed, raising the entry age to seven). The daughters of needy Masons were given the next priority.

2) Form of Petition.

Strict rules were laid down requiring details of a family's circumstances, evidence of membership of a Lodge by the father and a birth certificate. The application to the school was called a Petition and all the cases were considered before a Petitions Committee. (These conditions still applied when Mother wanted my application to be considered).

Purpose of the Institution:

i) To preserve the Female offspring of indigent Freemasons from the dangers and misfortunes to which their distressed situations may expose them.

ii) To train young female minds destitute of parental care and attention to industry, virtue, social and religious duties.

iii) To qualify the children to occupy a useful though not menial situation in life. (We were encouraged to think of training for a career in the nursing, teaching and secretarial professions).

There were a total of thirty three rules, including the correct procedure for changing bed linen, clothes washing, personal hygiene and how to polish shoes. The girls' lives were highly regulated, starting with a bell every morning at six o'clock during the summer and eight in winter. After washing, they said prayers and had breakfast at nine. They had lessons until 'dinner' at one o'clock, one hour of free play until school ended at five, followed by evening prayers. Supper was at seven and bedtime one hour later. This routine had changed very little by the time I attended Weybridge in 1936.

The girls' menu included beer twice a day. This may strike us today as very odd, but a light beer was a common form of refreshment at the time, in place of water which was very likely contaminated. The pupils were also expected to do needlework to help pay for their keep. There were no full day holidays and the girls were prevented from having contact with other family members.

The rules were certainly strict, but the idea behind them was to make sure the girls had some kind of vocational education while receiving moral protection at the same time. This was particularly important during a period when the workhouse or worse still, prostitution beckoned and the risk of catching a disease like smallpox was very high. In spite of these worthy intentions however, a number of incidents occurred of family members trying to retrieve girls from the school through the use of force.

Later the rules were relaxed. We were allowed one visit a term from our mothers, who could be accompanied by a member of the family. I remember that my Grandmother and a cousin had visited me at Weybridge.

The Second School 1795–1853
St George's Fields

The school moved to St George's Fields sometime towards the end of June 1795 and the name changed to the Freemason Girls' School. Before long the number of pupils had risen from thirty to sixty in 1802 and two years later to sixty two. In London at the time, there were around seventy Charity Schools, serving as the model on which the Royal Cumberland School had been based. The Charity School movement had been steadily growing for about one hundred years throughout Britain at that time. But the main difference between what Ruspini had started and the others, was that he had obtained the support of men in high society who were wealthy. In this respect, Ruspini's project had many advantages over the other schools, enabling it to expand further and become the great school it is today. The education at the time though was very basic, consisting of reading, writing, arithmetic, needlework and domestic duties. A number of attempts were made to increase the subjects taught to include French and Drawing. In 1844, the school was presented with its first piano—a hundred years later there were many more!

The Third School 1853–1934
St John's Hill, Battersea Rise

Although called the Wandsworth school, it was actually located at St John's Hill, Battersea Rise next to Clapham Station. It is perhaps worth remembering that back then, the location was surrounded by open country and the air was healthy. During this period the Countess of Zetland was taking note of the girls' diets and exercise regimes, which were changed. The school doctor also insisted on three week vacations in the summer and winter.

The beginning of a new era resulted in the school modernising the girls' clothes. French, drawing and music were taught and two new pianos purchased. The library was also improved. All needlework was stopped, except for when it was necessary for the girls to repair their own clothes.

By 1859, the numbers in the school had risen to eighty and the leaving age was now raised to sixteen, which would have been a radical step for the times. Seventeen years later the numbers had increased to 148 and by 1881, there were 235 pupils. The desire to expand the schools premises continued unabated.

When 'The Titanic' sank in April 1912, the RMIG committee agreed that any daughters of Masons who had lost parents on the ship would be elected to the school without a vote. Twin girls were admitted in September of that year and two others at a later date. Also at this time, the headmistress decided that a modern education required properly educated teachers. She suggested

Report of the General Committee of RMIG: Income and Expenditure Account and Balance Sheet, 31 December 1898 (abridged).

Income	£	s	d
Donations & subscriptions	11,490	6	0
Grand Lodge	150	0	0
Grand Chapter	10	10	0
Total	£ 11,650	16 s	0 d
Special donations (Grand Lodge)	2,105	0	0
Interest on investments	2,482	7	6
Receipts on deposits & other	240	1	4
Total	£ 16,478	14 s	10 d
Expenditure			
Provisions	3,369	0	8
Salaries & wages	3,389	13	6
Clothing for children	971	18	6
Other	6,035	0	0
Total	£ 13,764	11 s	8 d
Surplus for the year	**£ 2,714**	**3 s**	**2 d**
Balance sheet assets made up of:			
Freehold land and buildings at Clapham	97,664	18	0
Investments:			
Consolidated 2¾% stock	68,374	5	6
India 3% stock	20,424	4	4
India 2½% stock	3,046	0	0
Total	£ 96,391	8 s	3 d
Total capital	**£ 200,417**	**9 s**	**7 d**

that an outstanding girl, after becoming a pupil teacher at the school for one year, should be sent to Goldsmith's College and that she would return to the school after completing her training. I became a pupil teacher and my first interview was at Goldsmith's, though of course I did not return to Rickmansworth after training and neither was I an outstanding pupil!

By July 1916, there were 668 girls receiving help from the Masonic Institution, with 350 of them at Clapham. The committee decided it would be a good idea to move the Junior school out of London. A year later a suitable site was chosen at Weybridge, which had originally been built as a boys' school. It was ready for occupation by August 1918. Twenty girls from Clapham immediately followed and before long they were joined by twenty five more.

By 1919, up to £600 was made available to any deserving girl who wanted to attend university, showing how far the school had come in terms of improving the standard of education. The initial steps to move the senior school out of London began as earlier as 1927, with the purchase of an estate owned by Lady Barrington of 280 acres for £61,500. The process of fencing off the grounds, preparing plans and getting architects bids began.

> Stage A: Eight school houses, £128,432.
> Stage B: Classroom block, Assembly Hall, £71,757.
> Stage C: Admin block, Chapel, Infirmary, £93,571.
> Names of the eight Houses: Ruspini, Zetland, Moira, Connaught, Sussex, Alexandria, Atholl, Cumberland.

Building work started and the foundation stone was laid in July 1930. To coincide with the construction of new premises, the school badge was redesigned. A five pointed star, or pentalpha formed the main feature with a smooth ashlar in the centre. Standing on a Masonic pavement, were two pillars, enclosed by a double golden circle, containing the school motto (from Psalm 144, v.12), 'Circumornatae ut similitudo templi,' or, 'That our daughters may be as the polished corners of the Temple.' According to Masonic symbolism, the two pillars represent the entrance to the Temple, which in Freemasonry is given the allegorical significance of building an upright and morally virtuous person as well as being the font of wisdom. The black and white pavement, the uncertainty of life, with its good and bad days, joys and sorrows. The pentalpha, with its five equal points, symbolises the five senses through which we experience life. It also has a number of other associations, including the five points representing the five wounds of Christ. The circle with no beginning or end stands for eternity. And finally, the smooth ashlar in the centre is considered the most beautiful element of all, the perfected form of the rough hewn cube that becomes the polished corner of the Temple.

By 1934, a total of 1,300 girls were receiving support from the Masons, with 275 of them at Clapham. The girls who could not be admitted, were out educated at other schools across the country.

The Fourth School 1934–present
Rickmansworth Park

Staff and pupils assembled at the new school at Rickmansworth in April 1934, and it was formally opened by Queen Mary on June 27 of that year. The total cost had reached nearly £300,000. It was made up of eight houses, each accommo-dated fifty children. There were 250 acres of playing fields and parkland, an indoor swimming pool, Chapel and gymnasium. The annual running costs of the senior and junior schools in 1934 were close to £90,000. Income from investments amounted to £13,000, with the difference being made up by subscriptions from individual Freemasons, Lodges and special festivals. When George VI became King in 1936, he agreed to act as Patron and every Christmas sent a donation.

Some doubts were expressed about the quality of the diet and the Medical Officer was asked to look into the matter. Although he found the calorie content was above the daily average (2,400) it was well below what was needed for growing girls, of around 3,000. There was also a protein deficiency and the school was asked to provide more interesting and appetising meals.

In 1938, the worsening international situation meant that the Masons were considering storing enough food to last a month. Gas masks were issued to all girls at Weybridge and Rickmansworth and trenches were built. And 1938 was also the 150th centenary of the school and brooches were presented. I have since thought how drab we must have looked on that occasion, in the dark blue serge dresses and brown cotton aprons, which covered us front and back. The move to Rickmansworth also brought with it another big change. The school uniform had altered little since the nineteenth century and significantly the girls were still required to wear pinafores, which were symbols of the old Charity School.

By 1934, Rickmansworth was unrecognisable compared with the first school Ruspini had established in Somers Place East. It was also thought that pinafores were no longer appropriate for the times (and none of us liked them anyway). So in 1939, as one of the first acts of the new headmistress Miss Calway, the pinafore disappeared. Later she married and asked to leave her job and in 1941, Miss Fryer took over the position. It was after this decision that we had napkins at meal times, and we embroidered a 'pochette' to keep them in.

Parents were told they did not have to send their daughters back to the school on the outbreak of war. But it was probably a lot safer, especially for any girls living in London and other major ports. Weybridge was closed and the girls transferred to Rickmansworth. For the duration of the war, Unilever became tenants at the Junior School.

At the end of hostilities, the entrance gates were replaced at a total cost of £850, with half the expenditure being met by the local authorities and the trenches were filled in.

Following the extension of the Welfare State in the 1940s, there was a lot of rethinking about the role of benevolent societies, whether they would be needed and how they would survive in a fast moving economic climate. As the years passed, changing social conditions meant that women were often a lot better off than in the pre–war period. New job opportunities and rising standards of living, reduced the number of girls who met the schools' strict entry requirements.

At the same time costs were rising, particularly during the bout of rampant inflation in the 1970s. It was therefore sad but inevitable, that the Weybridge Junior School closed in 1973 and for the final time, the girls moved to Rickmansworth.

The fundamental motivation of the Masons in establishing and operating these schools was not to give out alms or charity. Their guiding principle was:

> '… to put into the hands of these children the weapon of education, so they can fight for themselves and go out into the world to take up their positions, which their fathers would have given them, had they been able to.'

The Royal Masonic School for Girls today

Today, the Royal Masonic School for Girls, is fully independent and operates in the private education sector. While it still takes in Petition girls, it is also open to fee paying pupils of any denomination, whether or not they are daughters of Freemasons.

The School also has its own open scholarships to help less well off parents, so continuing to follow the principles and the original objects laid down by Ruspini and his fellow Freemasons, when they established the first school. These scholarships are in addition to the assistance given by the Royal Masonic Trust for Girls and Boys (see opposite). The ethos of the school remains the same as always—find the talents of the child and enable her to exploit these to the full.

In the period since the end of World War II, the Science Block, with observatory, the Library and new Sports Centre, called the Princess Marina Hall, have been added to the original buildings at Rickmansworth. In the last few years, extensive cabling has enabled the school to be fully equipped with computers. Many local sporting associations as well was national institutions, use the facilities at the Princess Marina Hall, assisting other charities and sporting organisations for the benefit of the community.

From the narrow basis of the original school, girls currently study (in addition to the usual 'GCSE' and 'A' level subjects), Business Studies, Health and Sociology, Performing Arts, Photography, Politics, Psychology, Travel and Tourism and Textiles. However, while the curriculum has changed with the times, the School Drill carried out to music, but without verbal instruction has continued. The playing of several pianos, each with three girls playing the score, is a major part of the music programme on Prize Day. So despite the passing years, tradition has been maintained. In the latest League Tables, the school is in the first 200. You can find a fuller picture of what the school offers girls today, on the website: www.royalmasonic.herts.sch.uk.

The Royal Masonic Trust for Girls and Boys

In 1982, the Royal Masonic Institution for Girls (est 1788) and the Royal Masonic Institution for Boys (est 1798) were combined, creating the Masonic Trust for Girls and Boys. The Trust has continued nearly two hundred years of benevolent work, caring for the children of poor families. In May 2003, the name was changed to the Royal Masonic Trust for Girls and Boys (RMTGB).

The Trust's prime object is, 'to support the children of distressed or deceased Freemasons, the aim being to give them the start in life they would have received had distress not befallen their families. The second objective is to provide help to children not connected to Masonic families and to support charities connected with children.'

These principles resonate strongly with the original aims set down in the constitution of the first school at Somers Place East in 1788. The Trust's headquarters are still at 31, Great Queen Street, London and its website is: www.rmtgb.org.

THE ADMISSION PROCEDURE
1934–5

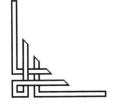

III: The Admission Procedure 1934–5

The rules for gaining admission to the Masonic School, were clearly laid out and very strict. If they were not complied with, then a girl would not be admitted. I think this was always at the back of Mother's mind whenever she had to deal with all the paperwork for my Petition.

Just because Mother was the widow of a Freemason with a daughter, did not automatically entitle her to send me to the Masonic School. But one way or another she was determined to get me a place, using friends and contacts she had made at the Methodists' Church at Waterloo to help her.

The following documents are the actual ones which log some of the correspondence she exchanged with the Secretary of my Father's Lodge, the 'Star in the East.' She had in fact been keeping in touch with the Lodge ever since my third birthday.

The first letter starts at the beginning of 1934 and the rest continue until July the following year, when my Petition was ready for presentation to the General Committee.

I was elected to the School on October 10, 1935. This must have come as a great relief to Mother, as now she knew I would be well looked after and receive the kind of education she did not have the means to provide.

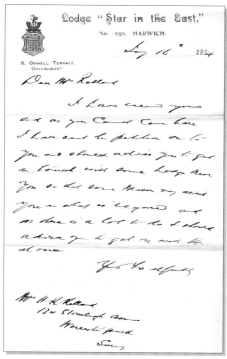

May 16th 1934

9, Orwell Terrace

Dovercourt

Dear Mrs Kelland,

I have received yours and as you cannot come here I have sent the Petition on to you and should advise you to get in touch with some Lodge near you so that some Mason may assist you in what is requested and as there is a lot to do I should advise you to get on with this at once.

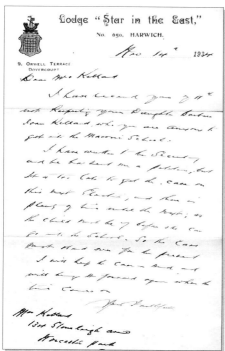

Nov 14th 1934

Dear Mrs Kelland,

I have received yours of 11th with respect to your daughter Barbara Joan Kelland, who you are anxious to get into the Masonic School.

I have written to the Secretary and he has sent me a Petition but it is too late to get the case on this next Election, and there is plenty of time until the next; as the child has to be 7 before she can go into the School. So the case must stand over for the present.

I will keep the case in hand and will bring it forward again when the time comes on.

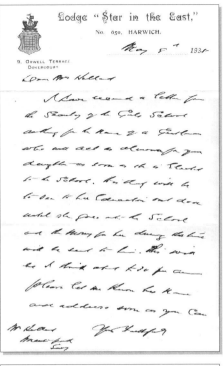

May 8th 1935

9, Orwell Terrace

Dovercourt

Dear Mrs Kelland,

I have received a letter from the Secretary of the Girls' School asking for the name of a gentleman who will act as Almoner for your daughter as soon as she is elected to the school. His duty will be to see to her education until she goes to the school and the money for her during this time will be sent to him. This will be I think about £30 per annum.

Please let me know his name and address as soon as you can.

July 12th 1935

9, Orwell Terrace

Dovercourt

Dear Mrs Kelland,

Referring to your letter of 11.11.34 re your daughter Barbara J Kelland, who you are anxious to get into the Girls' School, I have the Petition ready and I think the best thing you can do is to come to Dovercourt and see me so that we can go into the matter. I have been Secretary of this Lodge for 53 years and have got several boys* and girls into the School, so I am well acquainted with what is required.

I shall be glad to hear from you and with kind regards and best wishes.

*The Secretary was referring to the Masonic School for Boys, based at Bushey, Hertfordshire.

By kind permission of the Royal Masonic School for Girls

LEFT: letter approving Mother's Petition on my behalf.

BELOW LEFT: letter informing Mother that I had been elected to the Masonic Institution, without a ballot and I had been awarded a grant for out education of £25.

BELOW: some of the Institution's Laws, which parents had to observe if they wanted their daughters to be admitted to the school.

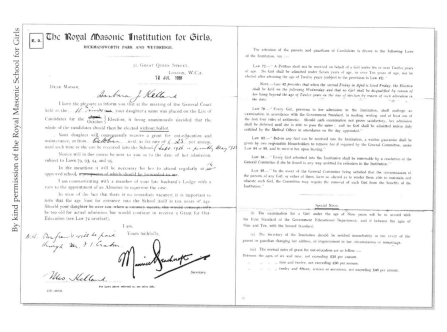

By kind permission of the Royal Masonic School for Girls

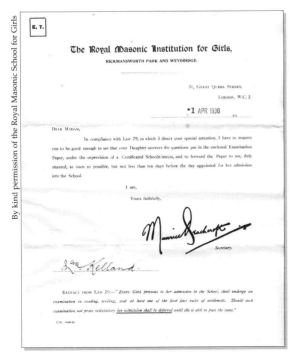

ABOVE LEFT: letter requiring revaccination and the names of proposed guarantors. ABOVE: conditions to be observed regarding revaccination and the possessions each girl was allowed to bring. LEFT: notification of school entrance exam paper.

By kind permission of the Royal Masonic School for Girls

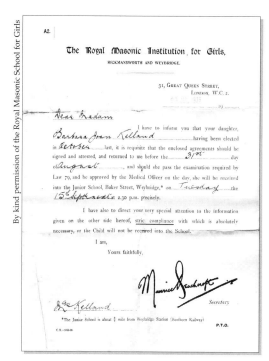

LEFT: the letter confirming my election to the school, subject to passing the medical and entrance exam!
BELOW: receipt for certificates. Mother was required as part of the admissions procedure to provide evidence of her marriage, my birth and my father's death.

By kind permission of the Royal Masonic School for Girls

274

A Short History Of
Freemasonry

IV: A Short History of Freemasonry

No one knows the exact origins of Freemasonry. But this has not stopped all manner of different theories being put forward about how it started. Some of these have probably become embellished as time has passed, while others may hold more truth.

The traditional version of Masonic history, claims to trace its origins not only as far back as the Middle Ages, when masons were building great cathedrals across Europe, but even further to the time of the Biblical Patriarchs, King Solomon and the construction of the Temple in Jerusalem, the Greek and Roman civilisations and the Ancient Egyptians. Although by the early part of the nineteenth century, Freemasonry's idealised past was being rejected in favour of a more down to earth reality about it origins, the idea that it could be traced back to the time of the ancient civilisations, whose leaders possessed a powerful and secret knowledge, has never completely gone away.

However, it seems reasonably clear that there was a connection between the medieval stone masons who practised the physical craft of masonry, and what is often referred to as speculative Freemasonry.

The Knights Templar

In 1737, the idea was put forward that Freemasonry owed its origins to the Knights of Saint John of Jerusalem, who brought the revived Order and ancient ceremonies back to Britain. The Order of the Knights Templar was founded in 1118 to protect pilgrims travelling to Jerusalem. When the crusaders were eventually driven out of the holy lands, the Order continued in Europe until 1307, when the Pope dissolved it in 1312, and its Grand Master was burnt at the stake.

One idea is that the Templars who survived, fled to Scotland where they continued to keep the Order together in secret, until it was strong enough to emerge as Freemasonry, the implication being that the Templars secrets were thereby handed down to the Freemasons. However, some historians dispute this version of events, not least because there was no persecution of the Templars in Scotland as the Papal Bull was not observed there.

Although there are similarities between the two orders they are probably nothing more than superficial. For example, King Solomon's Temple is revered by both. But the Freemasons treat its construction as an allegory representing the building of an upright and morally virtuous person and the font of wisdom, while the Knights just used it as a headquarters and place to keep their horses. However, the Templar Knights association has proved powerful and long lived. So a Masonic Order of Knights Templar exists, drawing on the association between the chivalry of the ancient knights and practice of Freemasonry. In addition, the Ancient and Accepted Scottish Rite of Freemasonry has adopted the symbolism of the Templars within its ritual structure.

The Three Stages of Freemasonry

The three stage development theory is based on the idea that Masonic lodges emerged as a result of a three step process: operative, transitional and speculative. The first lodges regulated the trade of masons who were building the great cathedrals, castles and abbeys of England. By the beginning of the seventeenth century these lodges started taking in men who were not stone masons. Eventually the new recruits out numbered the original members, and they turned operative lodges into speculative ones. This pattern of behaviour appears to have been first recorded in Scotland.

The philosophical origins of Freemasonry seem to have found their expression in the need for men to practice tolerance and openly exchange their opinions. Members only had to acknowledge the existence of a Supreme Being (which is still the case today), thereby allowing people of many different religious faiths to join an organisation free from both religious and political intolerance, united in a spirit of friendly co-operation.

A common method of teaching during the seventeenth century was through the use of allegory and symbolism. King Solomon's temple was used to represent the building of a better man in a better world and the masons' working tools became symbols of the organisation's ideals. Religious persecution was always present during the seventeenth century. The revocation of the Edict of Nantes by Louis XIV in 1685, led to French Protestants, the Huguenots, fleeing to England. Their prominence in the early years of the Grand Lodge of England, suggests they would have embraced the ideals of an organisation where religious tolerance was practised.

The Origins of the Craft in England, Scotland and Ireland

On June 24, 1717, four previously formed old lodges, met at a tavern called 'The Goose and Gridiron' near St Paul's Churchyard in London and constituted the Grand Lodge of England. Six years later the Grand Lodge's regulations were codified and together with the publication of a history of the Craft, gave rise to the establishment of Freemasonry in its public form.

After 1720, a cultural shift took place in Freemasonry. All Grandmasters were either members of the nobility or royal family and the Grand Lodge was increasingly associated with high society. By the middle of the 1720s, Freemasonry had expanded outside of London into the provinces, which increasingly accepted the Grand Lodge's jurisdiction, with the notable exception of York, where an independent Grand Lodge emerged.

Lodge is the Masonic term used to describe the building or room where Freemasons meet. In the early days of the Craft there were no permanent Masonic halls, temples or lodges and so meetings were held in taverns or coffee houses. The lodge room would have had a rectangular table at its centre, with the various properties of the lodge laid out on it. An oblong was drawn on the floor in chalk and it would enclose the symbols necessary for whatever ceremony was to take place. A candidate took an obligation to preserve the mysteries of the Craft, after which the Masonic word and sign were communicated together with the Charges, or undertakings the new Mason had given to God, his Master and fellow men.

At the beginning of the eighteenth century a two degree system of advancement through the Craft was established, and later a third degree was added. Certain practitioners who were known as the Ancients, developed a ceremony called the Royal Arch. Eventually this was incorporated into the Master Mason Degree, in a compromise move, which reunited the two rival factions of the Craft that had become separated between 1751 and 1813.

> First degree: Entered Apprentice.
> Second degree: Fellow Craft.
> Third degree: Master Mason including the Supreme Order of the Holy Royal Arch.

A Grand Lodge in Scotland did not begin until 1736, when thirty three lodges combined. A considerable operative element existed in Scotland and this led to tensions. In 1743, disagreements between members resulted in the Canongate Kilwinning Lodge resuming its independence—a position which lasted seventy years. During this time it supported other lodges in Scotland and North America. It was also involved in disruption to Scottish Masonry caused by the Jacobite Rebellion of 1745. The Kilwinning Lodge was Jacobite and particularly partisan. However, harmony was eventually restored when it became clear the rebellion had failed.

The first Grand Lodge was recorded in Dublin in 1725 and in Masonic terms it was a model of tolerance, with both Protestants and Catholics coming together. A leading patriot of the time Daniel O'Connell was active in Irish Freemasonry, until he resigned from the Craft, when mistakenly told that the basic principles of Freemasonry were at fault for the excesses of the French Revolution during the Reign of Terror. Relations with Rome were strained in any event, after the Pope issued anti–Masonic Bulls in 1738 and 1751. In the latter period of the eighteen century, a great exodus of Catholics from the Craft took place.

The Formation of the Ancients and Moderns

In 1751, a group broke away from England's Grand Lodge, concerned about the way the customs and rituals of Freemasonry were being changed. They joined a group of Irish Freemasons who because they were operatives and followed a different kind of ritual had not been admitted into any London lodges. The disaffected Masons set up a very active independent Grand Lodge and called themselves the Ancients, because they claimed to have restored the old ways of performing ritual.

Members of the original Grand Lodge of England, were now ironically referred to as the Moderns. The Ancients became a very strong competitor forming two hundred new lodges and they were recognised as the legitimate Masonic authority in England by the Grand Lodges of Scotland and Ireland.

The French Revolution

In the aftermath of the French revolution in 1789, Freemasonry was viewed with a large degree of hostility by detractors, who tried to claim that the Reign of Terror was a reflection of Masonic principles. However in England, when the Unlawful Societies Act 1799 was passed, with the objective of closing down dangerous and seditious societies, Freemasonry was specifically excluded from its terms. Increasingly, Freemasonry was being viewed as an institution concerned with benevolence and moral good. The old image of the fun loving Freemason, as portrayed by Hogarth had become a thing of the past.

In 1813, after sixty years of division, harmony was finally restored to the Craft by the union of the two rival lodges, the Ancients and the Moderns. New articles were drawn up and the United Grand Lodge of England was established. This seems particularly ironic when the idea of the original organisation was to breed a spirit of tolerance and brotherly love.

Certain changes were made following the reorganisation of the Craft, so that all overtly Christian references were removed from the rituals, thereby allowing non–Christians to join without compromising their faith. It was made clear that the Craft was not in any way attempting to challenge or set itself up as a new kind of religion. Indeed, it practised political and religious tolerance, providing a forum where men from different faiths could meet during a period when such a degree of open mindedness was hard to find.

Freemasonry in America

The oldest known lodge is St John's, in Philadelphia, which was established in 1731, and Benjamin Franklin is recorded as being a member. By the middle of the eighteenth century, lodges had proliferated along the eastern seaboard and up until the outbreak of the War of Independence in 1755, these lodges were run by Provincial Grand Masters appointed in England. During the war, sympathies were split between members of the Craft. Although only nine of the fifty five signatories of the Declaration of Independence were without any doubt Masons, many of the Revolution's heroes were or became Freemasons. Men such as George Washington, Benjamin Franklin, John Hancock, Paul Revere and John Paul Jones.

After the War of Independence ended in 1781, efforts were made to establish a National Grand Lodge but these did not succeed. Today lodges are governed by their own State Grand Lodge. In the early part of the nineteenth century a strong movement against organised Freemasonry grew up and several political candidates ran on an anti-Masonic ticket. Although this hostility eventually died down, it did significant damage to the Masonic movement in the north east of America.

In 1761, a Mason called Stephan Morin had brought the Scottish Rite to America. It offered a very different approach to the moral precepts underpinning the Three Craft Degrees. He developed what he called 'The Rite of Perfection' with twenty five additional degrees. Later a further eight were added bringing the total to thirty three. For close to seventy years the Scottish Rite in America followed a convoluted course with a great deal of chaos, especially in the north of the country. In 1853, Albert Pike rewrote the degrees, remoulding the whole structure. This change brought about a big growth in membership of the Craft.

American Freemasonry resembles two sets of stairs that begin and end together. The first step is the Entered Apprentice, the second, Fellowcraft, the third Master Mason. If he wants to go further he enters either the Scottish or the York rites. In the Scottish rite, a Mason climbs thirty degrees. Each degree teaches a moral and to earn it he must participate in a ceremony that dramatises it. In the York rite, a Mason advances ten degrees, referred to by name rather than number.

The Statue of Liberty

Benjamin Franklin founded the first subscription library in America and helped prepare the ideological framework for the American Revolution. The Masonic vision of liberty was first enshrined in the Constitution of the United States. It encapsulates the fundamental social principles of Freemasonry.

> 'We the People of the United States, in order to form a more perfect union, establish justice, ensure domestic tranquillity, provide for the common defence, promote the general welfare, and secure the blessings of liberty to ourselves and our posterity, do ordain and establish this Constitution for the United States of America.'

George Washington described Masonic principles in the following way, "I conceive them to be founded in benevolence and to be exercised only for the good of mankind."

Probably the best known of all Masonic inspired monuments is the Statue of Liberty. It was designed to celebrate the centenary of the American Revolution. The money to build it came from donations made by Masons in France and America, including the future President Theodore Roosevelt. When the cornerstone of the pedestal was laid in 1884, the Grandmaster of New York said, "No other organisation had ever done more to promote Liberty and to liberate men from their chains of ignorance and tyranny than Freemasonry." At the re–dedication ceremony in 1984 a plaque was attached to the statue, revealing to the millions of visitors the role Freemasonry played in the creation and construction of this global symbol to freedom.

> AT THIS SITE ON AUGUST 5, 1884, THE CORNER-
> STONE OF THE PEDESTAL OF THE STATUE OF
> 'LIBERTY ENLIGHTENING THE WORLD,' WAS LAID

WITH CEREMONY BY WILLIAM A. BRODIE, GRAND MASTER OF MASONS IN THE STATE OF NEW YORK, GRAND LODGE MEMBERS, REPRESENTATIVES OF THE UNITED STATES AND FRENCH GOVERNMENTS, ARMY AND NAVY OFFICERS, MEMBERS OF THE FOREIGN LITIGATIONS, AND DISTINGUISHED CITIZENS WERE PRESENT. THIS PLAQUE IS DEDICATED BY THE MASONS OF NEW YORK IN COMMEMORATION OF THE 100TH ANNIVERSARY OF THAT HISTORIC EVENT. AUGUST 5, 1984.

Freemasonry and the Nazi Party

Shortly after coming to power in Germany, Hitler began a campaign to eliminate organisations he considered enemies of the Third Reich. One of his targets was Freemasonry. As his armies swept across Europe, he made sure that all the newly installed Nazi puppet regimes, continued with the same policy.

In 1938, following the union with Austria, the practice of Freemasonry was outlawed and the records of Masonic Lodges seized. A year later, when Poland was invaded, the ban on Freemasonry introduced by the new Polish government was confirmed by Hitler. In 1940, the ban was extended to Belgium, Holland, Norway, Denmark and Yugoslavia.

After the fall of France in 1940, Pétain's Vichy administration seized all Masonic archives and transferred them to the Bibliothèque National de Paris. An estimated 5,600 Freemasons were sent to concentration camps during the Vichy regime.

In 1942, Hitler formalised the role of Alfred Rosenberg, Head of the SS unit operating in the Eastern territories, by issuing a decree in March of that year. One of Rosenberg's jobs was to organise the seizure of all Jewish and Masonic materials and have them transported back to Berlin. He also contributed to Nazi propaganda and produced an anti-Masonic book. The English translation of Hitler's decree is produced below:

> Jews, Freemasons and the other ideological opponents of National Socialism allied to them, are the instigators of the current war against the Reich. The organised intellectual struggle against these forces is a vitally necessary war task. I have therefore instructed Reichsleiter Rosenberg to carry out this task in cooperation with the Head of the Armed Forces High Command.

> His Operational Staff for the occupied territories has the right to examine libraries, archives, Lodges and other ideological and cultural institutions of all kinds and to have them confiscated for the ideological purposes of the Nazi Party and the subsequent scientific research work of the Hohe Schule.

> Cultural property, which is in the hands of or belongs to the Jews, is ownerless, or for which no clearly identifiable origin can be established, is subject to the same regulations. The regulations for implementing cooperation with the Armed Forces will be issued by the Head of the Armed Forces High Command in agreement with Reichsleiter Rosenberg. The necessary measures within the Eastern territories under German administration will be taken by Reichsleiter Rosenberg in his capacity as Reich Minister for the occupied Eastern territories.

The Hohe Schule, was to be the Nazi Party's cultural and educational research centre, comprising of a library capable of holding up to half a million books. Hitler intended for it to be built when the war ended so the enemies of the Third Reich could be studied.

By the beginning of the 1940s, Freemasonry was active only in three European countries, Britain, Switzerland and Luxembourg. It had already been outlawed by the new Russian Communist regime in 1924. Mussolini followed with a ban a year later and Spain's General Franco did the same in 1936.

When the Channel Islands were eventually liberated at the end of the war, a 'Black Book' was discovered, which amongst other things, listed the names of Masonic Lodge members in Britain who the Nazis intended to target once they had invaded the country.

Growing up in my protected environment at school, I had no way of knowing any of this was going on. I was very fortunate indeed to have been sheltered from such events. However in later years, I have often thought that had the Nazis ever invaded these islands, all of us at Rickmansworth would have been amongst the first to be rounded up and taken to concentration camps on mainland Europe. A very sobering thought indeed.

I would like to thank several people for their help and guidance in the writing of this book:

Mr K S Carmichael, CBE, Chairman of the Board of Governors of the RMSG, Colonel R K Hind, Secretary for the Governors, Colonel J C Chambers, Secretary of the RMTGB, Lorna Cowburn, Head of Library Resources at the RMSG, the Library staff at Freemasons' Hall, London, my Zetland House friends, who kindly allowed me to use some of their old photographs of our happy times together, and lastly—nothing would have been written without the support and encouragement of my family. Any mistakes or omissions are entirely of my own making and I apologise for them in advance.

Additional copies of 'This Time Next Week' may be ordered directly from the publisher by visiting the website site: www.eponamedia.com. There you will find information about the audio version of the book, resources relating to Freemasonry, more photographs of school life, as well as details of a Masonic tour of London.